T A L K I N G
TO
SPIRITS
IN MEDIUMISTIC
MEETINGS

TALKING TO SPIRITS IN MEDIUMISTIC MEETINGS
© Copyright 2016 by the United States Spiritist Council

Scripture taken from the The World English Bible (WEB) in the Public Domain, 1997.

ISBN 978-0-9852793-6-3
LCCN 2016945523
Proofreading: Jussara Korngold
Cover layout: Notleh
Book layout: H. M. Monteiro

International data for cataloging in publication (CIP)

O482t Oliveira, Therezinha, 1930-2013
       Talking to spirits in mediumistic meetings/ Therezinha Oliveira.
       Translator: Helton Mattar Monteiro. – New York: United States
       Spiritist Council, 2016.
       216 pp.; 22.86 cm.

       Original title: Conversando com os espíritos na reunião mediúnica.

       ISBN: 978-0-9852793-6-3

       Includes bibliographical references.

       1. Mediumship. 2. Spiritism. I. Monteiro, Helton Mattar. II. Title.

       LCCN: 2016945523   DDC 133.93   UDC 133.7

1ˢᵗ edition – June 2016

All rights reserved to
United States Spiritist Council
http://www.spiritist.us – info@spiritist.us

Manufactured in the United States of America

Authorized English edition by Editora Allan Kardec, Brazil.

THEREZINHA OLIVEIRA

TALKING
TO
SPIRITS
IN MEDIUMISTIC
MEETINGS

TRANSLATED BY H. M. MONTEIRO

**United States
Spiritist Council**

NEW YORK
2016

CONTENTS

PART THREE
EXAMPLES AND CASE STUDIES

INTRODUCTION

The dialogue with spirits is one of the practices we find in the Spiritist Movement, as a result of the knowledge we have of the existence of spirits and the possibility of communicating with them.

Such dialogues have always been taking place during countless Spiritist mediumistic meetings held daily throughout Brazil.

And the basic guidance for carrying them out derives from the information contained in the books of Allan Kardec's codification.

From said constant and usual dialogues, some valuable experience is gained about transcendental life, which Spiritists seek to record and share, so that everyone may make the most out of it.

Articles, comments, seminars, courses and books have placed within the reach of those interested in practicing the interchange with the afterlife, suggestions on how to conduct the mediums' work and attend to communicating spirits.

Such was the purpose of my previous books *Mediumship* and *Mediumistic Meetings*. In the latter, I had the opportunity of examining "The Dealing with Spirits," in one of its units.

Based on that unit, our Spiritist Center[1] has annually held a "Course for Dialoguers" which aims to prepare fellow associates to attend to communicating spirits.

Many such associates had repeatedly asked me to put that course in writing. This is what I am doing herein, having also further developed its subjects.

Part One of this book examines what the dialogue with spirits is, its purposes in light of Spiritism, and who takes part and intervenes in it.

In Part Two, it was essential to include some initial grounding in the dealing with spirits, for readers who had no access to the previous book.

In Part Three, the theme has hopefully been enriched by some examples of fruitful conversations with the spirits, from a selection of many dialogues held in our Center throughout the years.

Bringing no major changes nor greater novelties, this book now offers all I could draw from the existing Spiritist literature on the subject, as well as from our persevering practice of the dialogue with spirits.

Should this book be of some interest to those already at work in the blessed task of talking to spirits in the Spiritist Movement, as well as to those wishing to start out in this field, then for the writer it will have been a job well done.

---

1 Centro Espírita Allan Kardec, in Campinas – SP, Brazil.

PART ONE
PRELIMINARY CONSIDERATIONS

1

THE DIALOGUE WITH SPIRITS

Those willing to have a dialogue with spirits do it because they understand and accept that the latter exist and can communicate with us.

Spirits are intelligent beings created by God, which inhabit the universe as incarnate beings or otherwise.

Some people think that disincarnate spirits cannot communicate nor exchange ideas with us. About this, the spirit instructors replied to Kardec:

> But why should they not do so? What is a man, if not a spirit imprisoned in a body? And why should not a free spirit be able to hold converse with a spirit in prison, just as a free man can converse with another who is bound in chains?[2]

Yes, we spirits, whether incarnate or not, do communicate with one another. We are always in communication, be it through thought transmission (telepathy), or fluidic emanations which we constantly emit and receive.

One way or another, we all feel the influence of disembodied spirits, thus we can say that we are all mediums. However, this habitual communication usually occurs in subtle ways, and we do not always become aware of it.

---

2 *The Mediums' Book*, Part 1, Ch. I, 5.

In mediums, properly speaking, mediumship is well characterized by manifest phenomena which occur frequently and regularly.

That is so because, in mediums, an organic condition enables an expansion of the perispirit, and in such state of spiritual expansion, he or she regains functions of spirit, seeing and hearing what happens on the spiritual plane (which is invisible to our corporeal senses), and comes into contact with spirits which are freed from flesh.

Mediums convey what they perceive on the spiritual plane, and what they receive from the communicating spirit. The fidelity of transmission will depend on the greater or lesser ability of a medium to perceive and understand the reality of the spiritual plane, and what the communicating spirit is saying.

Despite some drawbacks in the process of mediumistic communications, it is through mediums that spirits "resurrect," resurface spiritually, and manifest themselves to us.

Spirits' communications and the Bible

There are those who claim that the Bible forbids communication with the dead. Let us recall with Jesus: *Now he is not the God of the dead, but of the living, for all are alive to him.*[3] Therefore, mediumistic communications are not with the dead, but with immortal spirits that animated bodies on Earth and, freed from them, keep on living in the afterlife.

---

3 Luke, 20:38.

In the New Testament, there is nothing about such a ban. Rather, Jesus used mediumship, taught it in theory and guided his disciples in the practice of mediumistic exchange. So much so that it was usually practiced among early Christians, as attested in the writings of the apostles.

In chapter 12 of his 1st Letter to the Corinthians, the Apostle Paul writes:

Now concerning spiritual things (i.e. the mediumistic faculties), brothers, I don't want you to be ignorant.

Because prior they were led away to mute idols (statues which spoke nothing), but entering the Christian Movement, they would encounter the practice of exchange with the afterlife (in which, though invisible, the spirits speak to us) and, to begin with, needed to know the following:

- *There are various kinds of gifts* (different kinds of mediumistic faculties) each causing a kind of phenomenon, *but the same God, who works all things in all* (said communications obey divine laws and designs);

- They would need to distinguish the good from the evil or ignorant communicating spirits, by examining what they said.

The evangelist John confirms this recommendation, with his advice in Chapter 4 of his 1st Epistle:

Beloved, don't believe every spirit, but test the spirits, whether they are of God, because many false prophets have gone out into the world.

The providential goal of such dialogues

Although we should take care and precautions when exchanging with the afterlife, it is beyond doubt that talking to the disincarnate, through mediumship, may prove to be very enlightening and beneficial; nor could it be otherwise, since it is our wise Creator and loving Father's providential design.

For the dialogue between "the living" and "the dead" to be really fruitful, it is necessary for us to have some knowledge about the nature of the communicating spirits, their given condition in the afterlife, and for what purpose God allows us to exchange with them.

There are those who employ the dialogue with spirits for research, as they seek to respectfully know the afterlife; whereas others do it out of mere curiosity or for various, not always advisable, interests.

In a Spiritist Center, however, – which is a temple, a hospital of souls, and a spiritual service workshop – the primary purpose of such dialogue is the one providentially set by God: to enlighten, comfort and fraternize with humans, incarnated or not, promoting their moral progress.

> You must never forget that the essential and exclusive object of Spiritism is your moral amelioration; and that it is for the attainment of this end that spirits are permitted to initiate you into the knowledge of the life to come, thus furnishing you with examples which you may turn to your own profit.[3]

Why through mediums?

In the quote above, there lies the answer to a frequently asked question:

Why do the disincarnate communicate through mediums? On the spiritual plane where they are, are not there other spirits that they could talk to and be understood by?

Yes, spirits already freed from flesh may, in the afterlife, talk to most spirits leaving the earthly world, in order to assist them on their arrival and referral in the spiritual world. Only a smaller portion of disincarnate spirits will communicate with us; and such exchange is providentially aimed at our moral edification.

The communication through mediums is also necessary for the moral edification of the disincarnate that have difficulty in assimilating the thoughts of the spirits, for, as the spirit instructors explain...

Our thoughts have no need to be clothed in words in order to be understood by spirits, for all spirits perceive the thought which we desire to communicate, through the mere direction of that thought towards them, and they perceive it in the ratio of the development of their own intellectual faculties.

In principle this is so, but...

(...) such and such a thought will be understood by such and such spirits, because their own advancement enables them to understand it, while that same thought will not be perceived by other spirits, because it awakens no remembrance, no answering consciousness, in their feeling or their mind, and is therefore not perceptible by them.

In these cases, the language of the incarnate is more accessible to such spirits because, when they link with the medium, and in the course of the mediumistic trance:

- They get rid of fluids that were disturbing them, and receive good fluids, thus enjoying greater clearheadedness and understanding;
- To some extent, once again they feel as when they were incarnated; seeing, hearing and perceiving as they used to in their former bodies;
- The way we talk to them is therefore familiar and usual to them and, for that reason, they better understand what we say.

Thus the dialogue with spirits through mediums, as providentially set by God, benefits both the incarnate and the disincarnate.

The Mediums' Book

It is especially through that book that Allan Kardec provides us with the Spiritist guidance for the work of mediumistic exchange.

That book really helps us to properly direct the activities both of the mediums and of people assigned to talk to communicating spirits.

In it, we learn that mediumistic exchanges should only be practiced as follows:

- *With high purposes*, thereby assuring us to attract the presence and protection of good spirits;
- *With reasonably healthy and levelheaded people*, as a well-guided mediumistic work should require;
- *Leading the mediums to operate with love, discipline and doctrinal knowledge*, without which they will not become proper instruments for the good;
- *Conducting meetings privately*, not in public, for the ambience may also influence the phenomena and, if unprepared, such influence may be detrimental.

We also learn *what may influence a communication*:

for a communication to be good, it must come from a good Spirit;

for the good Spirit to be able to transmit it, a good instrument is indispensable;

for the good Spirit to be disposed to transmit it, the pursued intent must be a suitable one. (*The Mediums' Book*, Part Two, Ch. XVI, 186)

As we can see, Spiritism offers a wealth of information on the dialogue with spirits, some of which I would like to share with the reader.

That is the reason and opportunity for this book, which makes no vain pretense of exhausting so vast and transcendental a subject, yet hopes to provide those interested in the topic with some contribution from all that the Spiritism has to offer.

2
How Kardec conducted dialogues

Through various mediums, Kardec held countless dialogues both with higher spirits and lesser categorized ones.

The way Kardec conducted himself while talking to them remains a model of how such dialogues can be efficient and productive.

Acting with patience and perseverance, order and method, Kardec knew how to draw valuable information from that interchange, managed to codify the Doctrine[4] as revealed by the Spirits and, with his teaching ability, made it accessible to the general public.

Thanks to the fruitful dialogues that he held with the spirits, today we can benefit from the vast knowledge contained in his basic works: *The Spirits' Book, The Mediums' Book, The Gospel according to Spiritism, Heaven and Hell, Genesis,* and also in his *Posthumous Works.*

Interested in conveying to others some guidance for a successful dialogue with spirits, Kardec was careful to clarify the following in various chapters of *The Mediums' Book,* and in the July 1859 issue of *The Spiritist Review.*

---

4 [Transl. note] Though the word *doctrine* has generally been avoided in this book due to its perceived negative overtones in English, its use remains perfectly legitimate when referring to a body of thought and practices, such as in Allan Kardec's French originals.

Spirits' communications (...) *can teach a great deal,* (...) *provide a powerful element of...*

interest (by making known the condition of the world which awaits all of us, of which at times we have extravagant ideas)

morality (as we see in them our future fate)

conviction (such intimate conversations offer us manifest proof of the existence and individuality of spirits, which are none other than their own souls detached from earthly matter).

"Spirits do not come according to our whim, nor do they reply to everything that takes our fancy to ask from them. With beings from beyond the grave, care and attention are needed, and knowing how to use language appropriate to their nature, their moral qualities, their intelligence degree, and the rank they occupy. (...)"

With them, we should be "dominating or submissive, according to the circumstances, compassionate with those who suffer, humble and respectful with highly evolved ones, firm with the bad and the stubborn who only subjugate those who listen to them with complacency."

Kardec has concluded that "the manner of talking to the spirits is therefore a veritable art which requires tact, knowledge of the ground we walk on, and represents practical Spiritism, properly speaking."

He recommended that, when talking to spirits, we "venerate those who are worthy of our veneration; (...) be grateful to those who protect and assist us; and (...) treat all others with the kindness and forbearance that we may some day need for ourselves." (*The Mediums' Book*, 280)

By looking into the dialogues that were recorded in his books (not all of them were), we realize the extent of evangelical and doctrinal knowledge, clearheadedness and brotherliness with which Kardec conducted them, attending to both the spirit instructors and the needy or rebellious spirits; enlightening himself, and enlightening us.

Let us learn from him the sublime, spiritual art of the dialogue with spirits, and exercise it devotedly in the labors of the Spiritist Center. Surely, observations, Spiritist studies, and a practical knowledge of human beings will greatly contribute to our acquiring the secrets of talking sympathetically to spirits; but only after prolonged apprenticeship will we attain the necessary degree, as achieved by the Codifier.[5]

࿇ ✿ ࿇

In order to judge of spirits, as in order to judge of men, we must have learned to judge ourselves. (*The Mediums' Book*, Part 2, Ch. XXIV, Identity of Spirits, 267, 26)

---

5 Allan Kardec, who systematically codified Spiritism.

3

WHAT WE LEARN
FROM DIALOGUES WITH SPIRITS

The possibility of communication with spirits through mediumship is a wise divine providence, so that we, although incarnated, do not remain confined only to material life, which could disturb us and hinder the march of our spiritual progress.

Thanks to mediumship, this divine channel of communication, we can learn something more about transcendental reality, and give better guidance to our earthly life.

Making use of mediumistic exchange is like opening a window to observe the life beyond, while still feeling safe and protected by our bodily life. And what admirable knowledge do we get then!

Intermediated by mediums, those we thought to be dead present themselves alive on the spiritual plane, confirming their individuality not just by the appearance of their perispiritual bodies, as they show themselves, but by manifesting their intellectual and affective traits, thus forcing us to conclude that bodily death is not the end of life.

Mediumship gains greater value when we not only see and observe the spirits before us, but talk to them, thus beginning to reap invaluable explanations about the continuity of life in the hereafter.

How much have we to learn from this dealing with spirits, as wisely and providentially set by God!

From the contact with spirits in general, mediums tell us what they see and feel, what is happening on the unseen plane. And serving as intermediaries, they enable the spirits themselves to report what they are experiencing in the continuity of existence.

Then the following become evident: the situations of happiness or unhappiness with which the spirits are met in the afterlife are the just result of the good or the evil acts they practiced in their earthly lives.

It also becomes clear that the divine laws in fact render to each one according to his or her works, but without ever denying them new opportunities for recovery and progress in the spiritual life and through reincarnation.

As our understanding grows about life in immortality, we end up realizing what also awaits us there in the future, according to our deeds now. Knowing this makes us more cautious in thinking, feeling and acting in order to obtain better results for our lives, here or in the hereafter.

When the dialogue is with the good spirits then we, full of gratitude, get all the help and encouragement that we need and which they may be able to give us.

And, in turn, it is gratifying for us, under the guidance and support of spirit benefactors, to be able to assist communicating spirits in need of rescue, by clarifying, comforting, and helping them better conduct themselves in the spiritual life.

Whatever the state of the spirits, everything we learn by talking to them will always be useful in guiding our own conduct here and now, during this life as incarnate beings, as well as later, in illuminating what awaits us as disincarnate ones.

Guided by Spiritism, let us confidently exercise mediumship and learn how to talk to spirits, in order to draw all the valuable knowledge that we can reap through the exchange with the invisible plane, as providentially set by the wisdom and love of God.

Accept, of spirit-communications, only what is good, generous, rational, and approved alike by your intellect and your conscience. (*The Mediums' Book*, Part 2, Ch. XXIV, Identity of Spirits, 268, 17 [end])

4
COMMUNICATING SPIRITS

The spirits that communicate during mediumistic meetings are those which once animated human bodies here on Earth, and now find themselves in the errant state, that is, wandering in the spiritual world, in the interval between two incarnations.

They may be aware or not of their situation, and sometimes still feel attached to places or people.

As for their development level, they can be as well developed as the participants of the mediumistic meeting, or even more so, but they may also be less experienced and capable.

Various reasons have brought them into the environment of our meeting:

- Some of them have come simply because they are either usual companions of the people who comprise the mediumistic group, or have been momentarily attracted by any of its participants;

- Others have come spontaneously, eager to participate in our studies and experiences, in order to learn or cooperate in them;

- Some others have been brought in by the spirit mentors of the mediumistic work, in order to receive the aid and enlightenment of which they were in need;

- There also have been those which come wishing to disturb or hinder the work, for disagreeing with the objectives of the Spiritist mediumistic meeting, which are to give spiritual aid and enlightenment.

Whatever their evolutionary level and the reasons that brought them to us, we should welcome them all with the same brotherly love. It was not chance that brought them, but divine law; reason why the spirit mentors have allowed them to come. Between them and us, there will always be a spiritual connection and a beneficial and brotherly objective, something that we can do for them, some learning which they can provide to us.

In the light of Spiritist knowledge, we know that we will not be able to identify all the spirits that communicate in our meetings. Not all were well-known or prominent people during their earthly life. The most highly evolved are, at times, indistinguishable from one another for presenting highly and equally developed qualities.

Neither is it indispensable to identify them in order to welcome and accept dialogue with them. Unless the spirit presents itself under a very well-known name, someone famous, or as a personal friend, or a departed family member.

Even in such cases, we should check if the spirit is able to respond with clarity and, when formulating questions, we should use tact and brotherliness. Questions such as: "Your name?"; "Where did you live?"; "What did you die of?"; "Where were you buried?" would all be unnecessary and inopportune.

In general, *what matters* is not so much knowing the identity of the communicating spirit, but *their nature and the content of their speech, what their goal is in manifesting themselves among us.* Is it a good or an evil spirit? Is it enlightened and benevolent, or ignorant and with evil purposes? That is what we first need to know, when talking to spirits, *so as to determine how to treat and attend to them.*

In such an attempt, we may resort to *fluid analysis* (the impressions caused by their fluids on us, because good spirits produce positive and pleasant fluids), and also to *clairvoyance;* having good care, however, to examine whether the spirit is trying to deceive us with an outward appearance, and if there were any distortions in what the mediums saw or thought they saw.

When examining spirit communications, we may find two different sorts of situations: spirits contradicting themselves or wanting to deceive.

Contradictions occur when spirits make a statement and afterwards say something completely contrary to what they had said before, whether for not being firm in their ideas, or because they are lying.

There have been occasions when it was thought that some contradictions cropped up in the communications of good spirits; however, after more careful examination, it was found that said contradictions were only apparent and not real:

- The answer had been distorted by the misunderstanding of listeners;

- The spirit could not find resources to express itself well, or had no means to compare spiritual things with our world;

- Or yet, the spirit had to adjust its knowledge to the level of those who listened to it.

To clearly determine whether or not contradictions existed, it is necessary to study, carefully and at length, several communications from a same spirit.

A *deception* occurs when a spirit falsifies the truth, seeking to fool the medium and the assembled group.

To prevent deception, let us not ask of mediumship what it is not supposed to provide: Spiritist mediumship practice should only aim at that which is useful for the moral improvement of humanity.

When a deception happens, it is customary to blame it only on the medium. Indeed, there are cases in which mediums, for lack of vigilance, and for their vanity, pride, or some other moral failure, give an evil spirit an opportunity to produce false communications through them. But the medium is not always the one to blame. It may be that the group has also contributed to that occurrence, by wishing or expecting from the meeting the satisfaction of selfish and purely material interests, which led to the presence and communication of a deceiving spirit.

Also, it is usually asked in those cases: *Why did the spirit protectors and spirit mentors of the meeting allow the deceiving spirit to act like that? Why did they not warn us?* It was so because the medium and the group needed such alert signal in order to correct and modify, for the better, their wishes and purposes. Otherwise, they would have remained unaware of the inconvenience of their attitudes.

In case of deception, the medium or the group should not feel downhearted or discouraged. May they be more earnest in their faith, in good thoughts and deeds, so as to not be deceived with false communications, and thus become entitled to the assistance of the good spirits.

Ultimately, the security of afterlife communications rests in only accepting good advice and guidance, and in only doing good and not evil, whatever the speech of the spirits.

ை ❀ ஒ

Therefore, there is no formula which can ensure the identity and nature of communicating spirits, except through an analysis made with common sense and, especially, from the moral viewpoint.

Let us examine, in communicating spirits, the language they use, what they do, as well as the feelings that they inspire in us, and what advice they give us.

Thereby we will know what their nature is, how to deal with them, and whether or not to accept their ideas.

5
MEDIUMS

Mediums who serve as intermediaries for the spirits to speak to us were called simply *speaking mediums* by Kardec. However, nowadays it is customary to name them *psychophonic mediums*, or *psychophony mediums*.

For a medium to be able to properly channel a spirit's thought, he or she must offer, besides the necessary fluidic affinity with the communicating spirit, a mental attuning to the spirit's thoughts; and also possess the necessary sensitivity to perceive the spirit's feelings, and the moral compass to assess the spirit's purposes.

Such conditions are not improvised, but acquired by the study of Spiritism, the cultivation of the intellect, the improvement of conduct according to the standards of the Gospel, and by the exercise of attention to, and interest in, fellow beings.

Hence the need to prepare the candidates for mediumistic work, as guided by Spiritist principles and ideas, before we can place them in the active service of mediumistic exchange. And such is the endeavor of all well-guided Spiritist Centers, following practical instructions as seen below.

To properly channel the spirits, the medium must be capable and passive. (cf. *The Mediums' Book*, Part 2, Ch. XIX, 223)

"Does the spirit of the medium exercise an influence over the communications which he transmits from other spirits?

'Yes. If he is not in sympathy with them, he may alter their replies and assimilate them to his own ideas and propensities; but he does not influence the spirits themselves: he is only an inexact interpreter.'"

"Is it for this reason that certain spirits have a preference for certain mediums?

'Yes. Spirits seek for interpreters in sympathy with themselves, and able to transmit their thought correctly. When there is no sympathy between them, the spirit of the medium becomes an antagonist and produces resistance; he is an unwilling interpreter, and, as such, is often an unfaithful one. The same thing occurs among yourselves, when a message is conveyed through a careless, hostile, or unfaithful messenger.'"

Mediums should be advised to the following:

- Avoid becoming dependent always on the imposition of hands by the dialoguer in order to reach the trance state;

- Avoid giving successive, nonstop communications, having short breaks between each of them instead, so as to eliminate possible fluidic residues and impressions which may have remained in your mind;

- Limit the number of communications in each mediumistic meeting, as determined by the meeting director;

- Return to your normal state by yourself, after each communication, instead of depending always on the dialoguer's help, which may still be given when necessary.

Despite such guidance, each medium has their own natural limitations. It is incumbent upon them only to offer themselves in a brotherly way to the communication of spirits, with all they can, and with no other purpose than to serve, according to the divine plan, for the progress of humanity and their own; without charging for anything, *freely giving what they have freely received.*

By utilizing the mediums' passivity, more experienced spirits will draw the best possible results from their mediumistic faculties, while less capable ones will manifest themselves in whatever way they know or can, nevertheless enjoying the same blessed exchange.

Notwithstanding any "imperfections" in such human telephony, by the end of the communications the actual presence of disembodied intelligences next to the mediums will be evident, in phenomena which prove the existence and survival of spirits, thus enlightening and comforting many.

The preservation of each communicating spirit's individuality, intellectual heritage and affectivity will also have been demonstrated.

And it will be seen that, in the afterlife, without any damnation, the spirits can always resume the unceasing march of progress, heading for the conquest of their intellectual and moral perfection, and hence advancing on the path which will consolidate their true happiness.

6

DIALOGUERS AND THE MEDIUMISTIC GROUP

In the Spiritist Movement the term *indoctrinator* is still in current use to describe any person who, in a mediumistic group, is charged with talking to the communicating entities. Such designation is perhaps not the best one, because no spirit can possibly be "indoctrinated" in a brief conversation of a few minutes' duration (as a dialogue in a mediumistic meeting usually is). To teach a philosophy, by explaining and convincingly arguing its principles, a much longer time would be needed.

The Spirit André Luiz in his book *Disobsession*,[6] channeled by Francisco C. Xavier, came up with the expression *counseling medium*, because the spiritual mentors' operations and assistance converge towards that person while attending to the spirits which present themselves at the meeting.

However at our Spiritist Center,[7] by general consensus of its associates, we have decided for the term *dialoguer*, while also seeking to appoint fellow members who are qualified for this task.

---

6 [Trans. note] Synonymous with "deobsession."

7 Centro Espírita Allan Kardec (in Campinas – SP, Brazil).

Qualities needed for the dialoguer

In principle, the qualification to be a dialoguer comprises the following:

- *Knowledge of Spiritism,* so as to know how to understand and attend to each communicating spirit, within their evolutionary level and according to the need of the moment;

- *Moral authority,* which is achieved through good conduct, to the best of our capacities;

- *Faith,* which is the conviction of the spiritual realities, acquired through knowing and experiencing them; and

- *Love for fellow beings,* without which one will not be able to reach them in the sphere of feelings.

The preparation of fellow members for the task of talking to spirits should be done by providing them with doctrinal knowledge, encouraging them to Christian conduct and brotherly feeling, but also by giving them the opportunity to practice with seasoned dialoguers in service, in order to gain some experience before getting to the actual work.

When a novice dialoguer is not doing well in a dialogue, the meeting director may give him or her some guidance, speaking quietly in their ear.

As for the conversation's progress, there is no model to guide the dialoguer, for the spirits vary greatly in their evolutionary level, their condition in the spiritual world, and during the moment of the mediumistic exchange. With doctrinal knowledge and brotherly love, the dialoguer should seek to treat them as they present themselves, and according to what they need.

Here are some other desirable qualities a dialoguer might also have for dealing with the mediums and the communicating spirits:

- *Patience, sensitivity and tact*, to listen to, and try to understand, the communicating spirits;

- *Vigilance* at all times, so as to not deviate from the intended conduct and objectives of the dialogue;

  Note: Let it not happen that the dialoguer feels, for example, scandalized or intimately averse to a spirit, because it revealed itself to have been a criminal, a rapist, a homosexual, a prostitute or a pedophile; even an aversion to one who once was a politician is harmful because, if the spirit detects the dialoguer's thought or contrary feeling, it may react badly, thus impairing the opportunity of making a good dialogue. When, in such cases, the dialoguer fails to welcome the communicating spirit with respect and brotherliness, as he or she is supposed to do, our spirit friends often withdraw the latter immediately, and the mediumistic trance is interrupted.

- *Humility*, in order not to place themselves above the communicating spirits, nor lose their temper when faced with occasional accusations or aggressiveness from them;

- *Prudence,* so as not to cause unnecessary reactions from the communicating spirits, nor precipitate their stories or the events;

- *Serene energy* to restrain, when necessary, any excesses of communicating spirits, which might endanger the safety of those present or disrespect the dignity of the ambience.

Mediumship is not indispensable to the dialoguer's task. If a dialoguer happens to have mediumistic faculties, he or she may employ those which do not impair their necessary clearheadedness for the conversation with spirits, such as clairvoyance and clairaudience.

Let us not forget that before verbalizing doctrinal and gospel teachings to the spirits, we should seek to apply them in our own lives.

Benefits to the dialoguer

Jesus advises us to make for ourselves friends *by means of unrighteous mammon,* situations that sometimes we enjoy on Earth even without merit, so that *when we fail,* when we disincarnate, *they may receive us into the eternal tents,* in their hearts.

When making dialogue with spirits with sincerity and brotherly love, each time we attend to them is like sowing which will reap for us, immediately or in the future, friends in the spiritual life.

The group's influence on the dialogue

It is undeniable that each participant in the meeting exerts both a fluidic and spiritual influence over its ambience, with everything they think, feel and do during it.

For that reason, when forming a mediumistic group, care should also be taken in advance to doctrinally instruct and morally prepare its participants.

The following is required of them:

- Know to maintain high thoughts and correct attitudes at all times, but especially during the meeting;

- Neither fall asleep nor allow attention to wander from the meeting's objectives, contributing instead good thoughts and prayers to sustain the spiritual and fluidic ambience;

- During the dialogue, retain sympathy for the communicating spirit and stand in solidarity with the dialoguer, not wishing to make a dialogue parallel to the latter's, not even mentally, for it will cause harmful interference.

If conscious and well prepared to do so, the group will be the ideal means and furnish the necessary sustenance for the brotherly dialogue to benefit both the incarnate and the disincarnate with the blessings of light and love.

PART TWO
THE DIALOGUE'S PROGRESS

1

STARTING THE DIALOGUE

In a Spiritist meeting, in which participants are people knowledgeable of Spiritism and aware of the objectives of the mediumistic exchange, ambience preparation is usually done by reading aloud a page rooted in the gospel, followed by a simple but fervent prayer.

Then they all proceed in an atmosphere of respect and love, in the expectation of spirits' communications, which will take place under the guidance of spirit mentors, and in accordance with the laws of fluidic affinity and mental attunement which govern the connections between spirits and mediums.

Sometimes it is the communicating spirit which, via facial expression and bodily attitude through the medium, starts giving demonstrations of its presence and mood: normal, suffering, upset, confused, and so on. Or the spirit begins to speak, revealing the most diverse moods, such as in, for example: *Where am I? Oh, the pain! I don't want to stay here.*

Other times it is the medium who shows signs of being involved by a spirit (an attentive dialoguer should notice such signs), or starts offering passivity to the communicating spirit, allowing it to speak.

Initial words

Whether the initial demonstration is given by the spirit or the medium, the dialoguer will approach the medium and give a simple, courteous, respectful, and brotherly greeting. For example: *Welcome everyone who God sends our way.*

If the spirit, even though well received, has not yet decided to speak, the dialoguer should insist in a brotherly way: *We are at your disposal, ready to listen to you.* Or: *How do you feel? Do you want something from us?*

Upon this brotherly initial reception, the spirit's good will towards us may depend; its willingness to give us attention or not.

It is not appropriate to greet a spirit as we usually do among ourselves as incarnate beings: *Good morning, good afternoon, good evening,* because the spirit may not feel to be in the indicated time, or the matter of time itself may not even make any sense to it.

If, to the dialoguer, there seem to be signs of a spiritual presence involving a medium, which however is not actually happening, then the medium should naturally clarify that no involvement is taking place at that moment and, with the same naturalness, the dialoguer should accept such information. If in doubt, the dialoguer may pray asking the spirit friends for help, so as to ascertain if a communication is needed; and the medium will seek to cooperate.

Let them speak

In the beginning of the dialogue, we must learn to listen to the communicating spirit, so we can discern its kind, its intention, whether it is aware or not of its spiritual condition, whether it can talk clearly, what its background is, its motivation or reasons for presenting itself in our meeting.

Without this preliminary knowledge, we will not get it right on what to say to the spirit, or how to treat it, so as to make it feel we are sympathetic and can be useful to it, thus inspiring its trust.

Once you have realized the communicating spirit's condition or intention, you can then speak to it with confidence and a desire to serve.

What not to say

We should not say to all communicating spirits: *You have already died*, or *you have disincarnated*. We should only tell a spirit that it has disincarnated, when we realize that it can accept this reality with some serenity. Otherwise, the spirit will be distressed and disquieted for not knowing the spiritual life in which it has awoken, nor what is going to happen to it. Then the dialoguer will have to calm the spirit down and assure it that it is among friends, that it will be helped and that everything will be all right; but sometimes the dialogue may not even be possible any longer.

And there is still the possibility that the communicating spirit is not a disincarnate one, but only an incarnate one during an out-of-body experience. (Please check the example "A surprise in the hospital," in Part Three of this book.)

Nor should we tell the spirit, right in the beginning: *You're in a spiritual emergency room*, because it may not understand what we mean and even become disquieted: *Emergency room? So, I suffered an accident?* (Please check the misunderstanding it has caused in the example "Attending to a psychiatrist", also in Part Three.)

Attract the spirit's attention

There are spirits which present themselves as being sleepy: *Let me sleep...* But they are not brought by the spirit friends into our ambience to continue sleeping; on the contrary, it is for them to awaken and conduct themselves better in the afterlife. Let us then draw the spirit's attention to the place and time: *Do you know where you are? Please look around. Wake up, because we have something important and good to say to you.* Those are some of the ways to bring such spirit out of its drowsiness.

Other spirits are aware that they have disincarnated but, for having been taught so, hold the following belief: *I must remain asleep until the final judgment.* We may draw their attention by saying, for example: *Jesus did not stay asleep but resurrected. Life goes on and God wants us to be active.* We may also invite them to look around; if they are in condition to do so, they will see spirits in full activity, both rescuers and rescued ones. It may also happen that the spirit is presented with someone that they thought to be dead and yet is still active and well. That touches, interests and completely arouses such spirit.

We should not confuse a misleading and unproductive drowsiness with that sleepiness which a spirit may feel after the dialogue, when such spirit has already been rescued and relieved by the spirit rescuers. In this case, sleep is beneficial, restorative, and will facilitate rescuers to lead the spirit to the place designated for it.

In case of fixed ideas

Some spirits are still trapped in the situation in which they disincarnated, or some problem or situation that worries them, and they seem not to hear anything other than their own thoughts, which they keep repeatedly expressing.

Such is the case of a man who has disincarnated suddenly and expresses worries about his business; or a mother of little children distraught at having left them; an accident victim still feeling trapped in the wreck or under the rubble; or those who experience the same pains as when they disincarnated.

The dialoguer should seek to "break" that monologue, by asking appropriate questions and showing brotherly interest, or by drawing the spirit's attention to something else. The dialoguer may join in the "theme" of the communicating spirit, to then attract it to other angles or subjects.

When we do not succeed, despite our efforts, we should not keep "arguing" with the spirit, trying to make it change its impression of the ambience or situation which it thinks to be in. Let us take the conversation into another direction instead, to console and appease it. At times, the good spirits assist by bringing in other disincarnate entities known to the communicating spirit, in order to calm it down. Or they may make the communicating spirit hear a police car siren (if such spirit is still under the impression of being robbed), or see doctors and a vehicle similar to an ambulance (if the spirit had disincarnated in an accident).

In Part Three of this book, the reader will find examples of some approaches in cases like these.

When the spirit speaks in other languages

Occasionally, spirits show up expressing themselves, or trying to express themselves, in foreign languages.

They are not always able to do it in a satisfactory way because the medium would also have to know such language, either in this life or from experience in previous incarnations.

Incidentally, the apostle Paul, in chapter 14 of his first letter to the Corinthians, advises us that speaking in other languages will only be useful if we can understand what the spirit says.

Should the medium not offer conditions for the spirit to speak in the language it used when incarnated, we may do as follows:

- Request the communicating spirit to just transmit its thoughts, which are the spiritual language, so that the medium can express them with the words of his or her current native language;

- Ask the medium to seek to pick up just the thought of the spirit, then to convey what the communicating spirit means to say;

- Request the help from spiritual friends to solve the difficulty.

Curbing abuses

Although Spiritist mediums are disciplined and restrained when offering passivity to the communication of spirits, without raising their voices too much nor getting physically agitated, it may happen that a spirit will need to manifest itself more freely, unburdening itself and even gesturing, in which case we should not inhibit nor completely prevent such communication, though still seeking to keep balance.

If communications through a certain medium are always physically agitated, the problem is with the medium, not with the spirits.

In both cases, the dialoguer can speak softly into the ear of the medium, providing guidance as to the proper conduct and encouraging the necessary confidence in the medium.

The dialoguer should always curb any abuse by the communicating spirit which disrespects the integrity of the medium and meeting participants, as well as the dignity of the precincts, the spiritual work taking place therein, and also the discipline of time.

Picking up thoughts, an interesting phenomenon

Sometimes, the spirit hides itself, believing to be "only thinking" about certain things but "letting slip" its true spiritual standing because, being in a fluidic and telepathic connection with the medium, the latter picks up such spirit's thought and speaks out what it did not intend to reveal. At times the medium even speaks softly, as corresponding to what the spirit is thinking and not to what it actually wanted to say.

Then the dialoguer mentions what he or she has heard through the medium and the spirit is caught by surprise: *How did you get to know that?*

Such picking up of the spirit's thoughts by the medium helps the dialoguer to better understand the spirit and correctly conduct the dialogue.

Intuitions and spiritual help

Dialoguers may have their own intuitions when dealing with spirits, ideas drawn from the dialoguers' own store of experience, which suddenly crop up in their minds.

A dialoguer may also receive, telepathically or through inspiration during the dialogue, some information and instructions from the good spirits which operate within the ambience of the mediumistic meeting.

We should keep aware of such spiritual help and seek to merit it through an honest effort to better ourselves both intellectually and morally, and an interest in contributing to the progress of our fellow beings and always acting with prudence, humility and serenity.

Form of addressing

In Brazil, dialoguers once used to speak to the spirits using a form of address which in English would translate as 'thou' or 'ye' perhaps because they considered spirits to be "otherworldly beings," and believed it would be disrespectful to treat them less formally. Those were different times...

Such ceremonious treatment caused difficulties in the conversation because it required the conjugation of verbs in a way not usual to most people, and caused an unnecessary distance between spirit and dialoguer.

Nowadays we better understand that the spirits are the souls of people who lived on earth, people like us, only devoid of a body; and that to talk to them, we do not need any special form of address other than the respect and brotherliness due to all fellow beings.

By the way, a friendly spirit pointed out that the dealing with the spirits, whether they be needy ones or spiritual friends, *should be conducted with simplicity and naturalness,* flowing spontaneously according to the possibilities and needs, both ours and theirs.

One time we made the initial greeting to a spirit calling it 'brother' to which it reacted negatively:

"What familiarity is this? Treat me with more respect." That spirit, as someone conscious of his important position in social life on Earth, had not yet understood its condition as a disincarnate being.

When a spirit reacts that way, we usually explain that such form of address is not disrespectful, because in fact we are all children of God and therefore brothers and sisters.

In the case at hand, despite giving the above explanation, upon realizing that the spirit would resent this form of addressing and might become unwilling to talk to us, we did as the spirit expected and started calling it 'sir' – though always in a brotherly way – until it could accept a simpler form of address later on, when it was made aware of the reality.

2

DURING THE DIALOGUE

At all times when attending to a manifesting spirit, the dialoguer should remain attentive, understanding, discreet, and also talk as follows:

1. In clear and logical terms, in a language accessible to all present, and aiming that the counseling will be also beneficial to other needy spirits present therein, even if the latter do not always manifest themselves.

   It is not uncommon for a dialoguer seeking to attend to a communicating spirit to hear it say: *No need to explain, I'd been listening nearby and already understood. I'll follow on with them...*

2. Whenever possible, making comments about Spiritist and gospel teachings, but wanting neither to show erudition nor teach a lesson on Spiritism.

   As we have seen, the amount of time available at the meeting is limited and the spirit is generally not in a condition to assimilate further teachings, as would be called for if we were to convey any doctrinal principles to it.

   Some spirits, still attached to their incarnate creeds of times past, panic when hearing of spirits or Spiritism. Others will not accept that anyone mentions, or talks about, God, Jesus or religious ideas (of any religion whatsoever).

3. Combining feeling and compassion with reasoning. Dialoguers should not remain impassive as if they were mere spectators of events: They should make an emotional assessment of the communication, vibrate with the communicating spirit, suffer together with the spirit while understanding its difficulties and fears; but should not follow it in its emotional unbalance.

4. Trying to understand and not to defeat the communicating spirit, because a dialogue is not an quarrel. The dialoguer should study the spirit's personal drama with empathy, in order to understand it and help the spirit.

5. Avoiding impatience or contempt, even if provoked to acrimony or hilarity. Making the dialogue without any criticism, censure, accusation or judgment on what the spirit reveals. A dialoguer should also avoid violent words or attitudes, but should never adopt a "systematic sweetness," always seeking to be meek and mild, for it numbs the mind without renewing it.

6. Avoiding to engage in long controversies, which only make one lose time (precisely what some spirits want), or are a source of irritation for us or the communicating spirits.

7. Dosing the truth so that frankness is not destructive, nor hurt the spirit that is unable to receive it because it came for help, solace and counseling which can give it peace.

8. Not forcing the communicating spirit to make a decision, but explaining the value of the opportunity it is being given to decide, and what is of importance for it, its real objective as an immortal spirit. Also suggesting an attitude to the spirit, a way.

For example, we should advise but not demand that they forgive those who were their tormentors. We ourselves are not able yet to forgive minor faults of our fellow beings.

Length of a dialogue

Attending to, and making dialogue with, a spirit in a mediumistic meeting take varying lengths of time, depending on the state of consciousness of the communicating spirit, its inner mood, and the purposes that brought it into the meeting.

In the case of spirits that still do not know they have disincarnated, sometimes a few minutes of dialogue should suffice for them to awaken, become to a certain degree aware that they are being helped, and that everything will be fine.

At other times, the dialogue will last longer (around ten minutes), because it will not be for the awakening of a spirit which already knows to be a disincarnate being, but for advising it, causing the spirit to reason about why it is in its current condition, and what it should do to conduct itself well.

With spirit obsessors, the dialogue takes even longer, extending to up to twenty minutes, because the dialoguer then seeks to know and understand the spirit's motivation behind the persecution it is undertaking; and then argues and demonstrates that it would suit the spirit to modify its attitude which has been of no benefit to it, but, on the contrary, is only hindering and increasingly complicating the obsessor's situation in the spiritual life.

A dialogue should not take longer than necessary for the following reasons:

- There are other spirits awaiting to be attended to, and the meeting time is limited;

- The presence of needy spirits always causes some unpleasant impression, some emotional and fluidic exhaustion in the mediums, especially in beginners;

- The evil influence of spirit obsessors is particularly taxing on mediums, who then may need assistance in their fluidic restoration.

If the brotherly assistance needs to be continued, the spirit friends will bring the communicating spirit back again in later meetings.

Look out for this

1. Do not stand too close to the mediums, nor talk too closely to them, and also avoid touching their bodies, so as not to cause them embarrassment, dis-

ruption in their concentration, nor perhaps have magnetic and fluidic interference on them.

2. Do not neglect oral hygiene, since you will be speaking next to the medium's face. A mint in the mouth, just before dialogue, can help improve the breath.

3. Do not wear strong perfume because not everyone enjoys it and some are even allergic to it.

4. Control the tone of your voice. Let it be sufficiently audible, but not hurt the medium's ears, nor disturb other ongoing dialogues.

5. Simultaneously attend to two or more hostile entities – or those needy for help – only if absolutely necessary, and provided there is no detriment to the meeting's orderliness.

Making dialogue under Jesus' guidance

Attending to disincarnate spirits still beset by adjustment difficulties, and entangled in hatred, revenge and moral pains, requires painstaking conversation and sincere feeling.

Upon making dialogue under Jesus' guidance, we will...

- recognize all spirits as our fellow members of humanity;

- treat them unaffectedly and talk to them seriously about their needs, based on the Spiritist revelation.

Therefore, making dialogue involves...

- staying calm and prudent;

- relying on the spirit mentors' team;

- leading the needy spirit to enlightenment;

- training your heart in understanding;

- listening without criticizing;

- guiding without accusing;

- teaching without humiliating;

- counseling without demanding;

- comforting without lying;

- sending vibrations in order to accomplish it all.

While developing our skills as dialoguers, we must not neglect some basic requirements, such as: doctrinal understanding, love, forcefulness when needed, and our moral endeavors.

To make dialogue with the spirits is an opportunity to disperse darkness by promoting light.

The spirit of Wilson Ferreira de Mello
(Message channeled by Emanuel Cristiano
during a meeting held on 05/23/1997,
at CEAK, Campinas - SP, Brazil)

3
AUXILIARY RESOURCES

In the dialogue, besides the spoken word, we have other resources we can use and which will work much to our and the communicating spirit's advantage.

Prayers

Praying is one of them. With it we can connect to the currents of universal energy, directing them to the benefit of our brotherly desideratum, and attracting the cooperation of the good spirits, which join their forces with ours, intensifying them or supplying our deficiencies.

We often use it to assist in attending to the communicating spirits, to curb the most difficult among them, to soothe the suffering ones, and to open the channels of needed spiritual perception in the confused ones.

This should not, however, become a mechanical practice, nor is it something absolutely necessary each time we attend to a communicating spirit, because there are cases where one can attend to, and guide it well without the use of prayers.

Passes are also very useful

By concentrating, dispersing or directing fluids, the magnetic healing pass will benefit...

- the communicating spirits by
  - soothing the afflicted ones;
  - reinvigorating the enfeebled ones;
  - leading them to sleep and necessary rest.

- the mediums:
  - favoring the mediumistic trance (but there is no need to overdo the bestowing of hands nor bestow them over the medium throughout the trance);
  - mitigating the negative effects caused by evil presences;
  - restoring balance to them after a difficult communication (if they are not able to do it by themselves).

Suggestion and hypnosis

As a result of their fixation on certain states and ideas, some spirits have impairments in the mind and perispirit, such as sores, disabilities, deformities and conditioning. Such impairments were caused earlier by the spirit itself, or through the influence of evil spirits which dominated it and have since imposed that unfortunate fixation on it.

At mediumistic meetings we do not use the techniques known in psychology and medicine as suggestion and hypnosis. Instead, with simple commands and induction allied to other fluidic resources and the assistance of good spirits, we manage to combat such impairments, helping the suffering spirit to regain its normal condition or to at least get some improvement.

Examples: *No, you have no wounds like that anymore. You have received help and the wounds are healing. Yes, you were*

*disabled, but in the body. Now you're recovered, your arm is fine
and you can move it again.*

It is admirable to observe, then, the recovery made by the spirit and its happiness in feeling relieved or restored!

It is true that an immediate result is not achieved in all cases, for there are spiritual situations which will only in time be fully solved, according to the divine laws; but signs of improvement are always felt, because these spirits are already in a phase of receiving help and, for that very reason, were brought into our ambience.

However, the dialoguer should not try to influence the spirit, while attending to it, by telling it to proceed to some place on the spiritual plane – for example, a garden – on the pretext of making the spirit feel better. We are not there to create unrealistic images and sensations, but rather to work with what the spirit really thinks and feels. We should only make such suggestions when complying with higher inspirations, which correspond to realities on the spiritual plane.

Ectoplasm

Quite often, the improvements noted by the spirits in their perispirit are due to ectoplasmic action carried out by the good spirits with the help of a few fluidic resources offered by the common participants of the meeting.

If there is a physical effects medium present at the meeting, then his or her more abundant ectoplasm, worked by the good spirits, may serve to get the perispiritual recovery of a communicating spirit, even in cases where it may have suffered rather serious deformities, as in cases of zoanthropy where they present themselves, and feel to be, in bestial guises.

Of spirits which thus manifest themselves, affirming to be animals, to have claws, and sometimes howling, we must understand that they have not regressed spiritually; it is just the way they feel. Though currently unable to speak, they still are, and will always be, intelligent beings already in the human scale, able to feel, hear and understand us.

So we should always talk to them with respect, patience and love, assuring them that they are humans, not animals, and can regain their human form; that they remain under divine protection and were brought into our ambience to begin their spiritual recovery.

So that they exercise thought and feeling, we may suggest memories of their childhood, their parents, maybe remind them of sunshine and blue skies, flowers and birds. Those are basic emotions which may awaken their human and spiritual condition.

It is exciting to see them change, the beneficial modification which must have occurred in their perispirit, because they demonstrate it by taking more human stances and attitudes, an early sign of recovery.

4
GOOD SPIRITS

Good spirits are characterized mainly by their moral qualities and constant willingness to help fellow beings.

Mediumistic meetings are occasionally attended by good spirits attracted by several factors: bonds of friendship with meeting participants; a desire to learn by observing the work in progress; a connection with the work being carried by the mediums present at the meeting.

However, at Spiritist mediumistic meetings, we must obligatorily have a special group of good spirits with specific functions, which we call *spirit mentors' team*.

Invisible but extremely active, said team directs the whole work of mediumistic exchange on the spiritual side as follows, for example:

- Selecting those spirits which can and should be attended to at a meeting, and through which mediums (taking fluidic affinity and mental attunement into account). Some of the spirits to be attended to, will have come along with the meeting participants, whereas others were the subject of our prayers and vibrations; most, however, will have been drawn to the meeting through various means – or collected where they are for the rescue they need – by the spirit mentors' team;

- Overseeing the attending to the spirits, controlling difficult communicating spirits, supporting the mediums, inspiring the dialoguers;

- Maintaining the order and security of the meeting, on the spiritual plane (on the material one, such duty belongs to the incarnate directors of the meeting);

- After the attending to the communicating spirits, releasing those which do not yet have the conditions for better assistance, with due regard to their free will; giving referral to those which need further assistance in sectors appropriate to them in the spiritual world; also restoring the overall spiritual ambience (on our material plane, the restoring of participants is a duty of the incarnate directors of the meeting).

Without relying on the presence and cooperation of such a spirit mentors' team, it would be a temerity to open a relationship with the hereafter. To earn such presence and cooperation, mediumistic meetings must provide favorable conditions for a brotherly and rescuing exchange.

Only pure and sincere objectives can justify the coming and the action of the good spirits among us.

Now let us look at some titles, commonly used to designate some of the good spirits which usually communicate in mediumship meetings.

Protector

We designate as *protector* a spirit which is attached to someone by affection and responsibility, and which seek to help, protect and guide, for the good of the assisted person.

Generally, the protector is just a benevolent spirit with limited knowledge.

If we were benefactors of humanity, missionaries of the Good, we would certainly have protectors to match. But as we are ordinary people, in order to help us, a spirit is not required to possess higher qualities.

Our protector, however, always knows more than we do, at least because, being freed from matter, it has a perception and knowledge which to us are veiled by the influence of our physical bodies.

In the dialogue with communicating spirits, we learn that there are spirits which *consider themselves* "protectors," *yet they are not,* for they lack spiritual conditions to that effect, or even a real understanding of their situation in the hereafter.

We should clarify such spirits, in a brotherly way, about their spiritual reality, stimulating their need to improve and be prepared, so that then, if necessary and allowed, they can help the person they are fond of.

Guide

Regarding mediumistic meetings, a guide is the spirit which guides the work of a medium, a work which influences the lives of other spirits, whether they be incarnate or not.

It must have more knowledge than its protégé about the task in which it will guide him or her.

Certainly any person who in this earthly life has a task which, regardless of not being mediumistic, affects other people's lives, such as medicine, the government of a people, and so on, will also have a guide for that activity of general interest.

Mentor

It is a spirit which gives help, protection and guidance, not only to one person, but to a whole group or institution.

It should probably be a Higher Order Spirit (also known as Superior Spirit) of the 2nd class, as listed by Kardec, combining wisdom with goodness.

Because of their higher order, such spirits are more apt than others to provide exact notions about things of the incorporeal world, within what is permitted for humankind to know.

Veritable technicians of the difficult science of the soul, their work is quiet and serene, and their names sometimes unknown.

They inspire through intuition, teach by example, and hardly praise anyone.

They advise, suggest, rectify, stimulate; never dictate norms nor interfere with our free will, because they do not want us to become their dependents.

They do not require from us any rites, rigid and irreplaceable formulas as determined prayers, mystical symbols, special garments, etc.

Rescuers

These are median spirits which form spiritual teams under the guidance of the higher spirit mentors. They rescue spirits in need, whether incarnate or not.

In this role of helping those who suffer pains greater than their own, they themselves also find the help they need, as ensured by the divine law of brotherliness.

Our attitude towards all of them

When good spirits manifest themselves in our mediumship meeting, we should do as follows:

1. Listen carefully to what they have to say to us, examining their ideas, asking the necessary questions to remove any doubt as to the meaning of their message;

2. Seek to meet their good guidelines; not following them would be losing an opportunity to err less and succeed more.

3. Do everything in our power to cooperate with them, because they do their part but we can also work together for the good of everyone and everything.

4. Thank them for their presence and help, in order not to be ungrateful, and encourage them to continue in their worthwhile and beneficial work to humankind.

5
EVIL SPIRITS

They are those which have not yet discovered goodness. They form a gradual scale ranging from the simply irresponsible to the consciously evil.

However, these are not demonic beings created apart from humanity, but rather the souls of people who, when incarnated, were frivolous or malevolent and continue to be so on the spiritual plane, because they do not want, or could not, improve morally.

Despite the state in which they appear, they are also God's children and our fellow beings. And God wants them too to have the opportunity of receiving the help and counseling they need; even if sometimes they do not understand such counseling and help; even if they do not seem to want them, or oppose resistance to them.

For safety, when dealing with evil spirits, we should just not let them influence us malevolently, instead influencing them with beneficial and brotherly actions.

Joking, mocking and playful spirits

When they are communicating with us, we may even find them amusing; but we should not let them take over the meeting's ambience, which has serious spiritual goals.

We must be vigilant, warning them of the bad consequences of their sowing and their frivolous behavior, while trying to call them to account.

If they do not want to heed us, we should seek to drive them away until they are willing to change their attitude.

Sarcastic, skeptical and materialistic spirits

With these, it is no use trying to discuss Spiritist teachings, nor engaging in polemics.

We should use a brotherly and firm approach, making them feel what truly suits them best as immortal spirits, and what they are missing because of their wrong attitudes.

Let us make dialogue with them up to a certain time limit during the meeting, and for as long as we see some possibility that they may accept our argumentation. Should they not be willing to change, or make good use of it, we will invite them to move away.

Deceiving spirits

These are spirits which distort the truth, pretending to be what they are not: a friend or acquaintance of the participants, a protector, a spirit of light, a famous person.

Even if there seems to be nothing bad in their message, why sign it under a name which is not theirs?

Sometimes they can produce some phenomenon, trying to better impress us.

Usually, they also do the following:

- Flatter dialoguers, mediums and participants; encourage vanity and pride, because they want to captivate in order to dominate;

- Throw (in between the lines of their communication) hoax and intrigue, trying to sow animosity and division among the members of the group.

Sometimes, even though unmasked, deceiving spirits will insist on manifesting themselves again in one or subsequent meetings, each time assuming a different personality, always fake ones, to keep fooling us.

In such cases, we should instruct the medium to try to avoid, if possible, offering renewed passivity to the deceiving spirit, if the medium again senses the latter's presence and fluids.

Overall, our attitude towards deceiving spirits should be one of vigilance, attention to examine their communications, patience with their behavior, and firmness in dealing with them.

We should listen to what they say, examining it and asking questions; "giving them rope," as it were, to check if what they say matches who they claim to be, or falls into contradiction.

If a deception is proven, let us not be hostile to such spirits, but instead vigorously argue that they themselves are the most fooled by their own attitude; and also insist on the invitation for them to change themselves.

In the extreme case where their communications become disturbing to the ambience, and they are not willing to change themselves, we may pray for spiritual protection to move them away.

Time-wasting spirits

The mediumistic meeting has a set time to start and finish. At the end of such period, the spirit mentors' team, which gives us security, will have to withdraw to tend to other tasks elsewhere and on other planes.

Knowing this, some spirits try to linger or manifest themselves when the meeting is almost over, thus hoping to disrupt the ambience and perhaps cause panic in inexperienced participants.

To prevent something like that from happening, we should never allow that the allotted meeting time is needlessly exceeded at the communicating spirits' initiative, or for our lack of vigilance.

What to do to ward off evil spirits?

The best way of expelling bad spirits is to attract good ones.

Be always good, and you will have only good spirits about you (*The Mediums' Book*, Part 2, Ch. IX, 13).

6
SUFFERING AND PERTURBED SPIRITS

How a spirit feels after disincarnating
The Mediums' Book, Part 2, Ch. 1, 53:

If we observe people attentively at the moment of their death, we find that their soul is in a state of confusion; their perceptions are muddled; they see their bodies, whole, or mutilated, according to the manner of their decease; and, at the same time, these souls see themselves, and feel that they are still living. Something tells them that the body lying there is *their* body, and they feel a difficulty in comprehending how it can be that they are separated from it.

They continue to see themselves under their previous form, and this sight produces in some of them, for a certain period, a singular illusion, viz., that of believing themselves to be still in the flesh. They have to gain experience of their new state, before they can become convinced of its reality. When they have got over this first moment of perplexity, they learn to look upon their corpse as an old garment which they have slipped off; and are not sorry to be quit of. They feel themselves to be lighter, and to have dropped a burden; they no longer suffer from physical pains, and are delighted with their power of rising into the atmosphere and gliding through space, just as, when in the body, they have often done in their dreams.

Meanwhile, notwithstanding that they have lost their body, the souls retain their personality; they retain their human form, but a form which neither troubles nor embarrasses them; and they also retain the consciousness of their *self,* and of their individuality.

Enlightened by Kardec's Codification, we therefore know that, in the spiritual world, there are spirits which feel in a state of unbalance and suffering for the following reasons:

1. They have not yet realized that they disincarnated; or they were not expecting to disincarnate just now; or they were not prepared for this. So they feel confused, anxious and frightened.

2. They are still impacted by the evils which led to their discarnation (illness, accident, etc.); or problems which make them suffer (resentment, attachment to what they left behind, drug effects, etc.).

3. They did wrong in this world and now, in the hereafter, are facing the consequences of their mistakes, experiencing remorse, nonacceptance and rebellion. Others experience fear to find themselves persecuted by those whom they had harmed on Earth.

We have the following as examples of suffering spirits in the hereafter: accident victims, murder victims, suicide victims, alcoholics, drug addicts, murderous despots, the demented, the avaricious, the selfish, the lazy, and materialists attached to physical sensations.

They needed to make contact through the mediums and be in the meeting's ambience in order to...

1. Listen and feel as they were not being able to do it on the spiritual plane, for lack of preparation and adaptation to the way of perceiving life without a body, through the perispirit.

2. Pass through a filter and renewal, both fluidic and mental, which the experience of mediumistic involvement can provide.

Our initial attitude

1. Offer them a brotherly welcome, listen with patience and tolerance; quickly seek information about what is needed to help them in the emergency in which they find themselves.

2. Provide them with first aid, with words that reassure them:

Example: *That pain will be relieved. It will improve soon. All this has passed, you're safe now, among friends. Calm down. Have faith...*

After getting some balance back in such spirits

Some suggestions of what we should check and how to act:

1. The spirit does not know it has disincarnated, nor is it in a condition to face this reality now?

If we have managed to release the spirit from the fixed idea which it was harboring, or if it calmed down, *let us then seek to deliver it to the care of the spiritual friends.*

The following may occur:

- *Spirit rescuers make themselves visible to them.* Sometimes we may even suggest: *Look to see if there's someone by your side.* Or *A friendly spirit will come to help you.* But there is no need to suggest it every time, nor keep insisting on that suggestion, because sometimes the spirit is still unable to perceive the spiritual plane well. However, even without seeing, the spirit can still feel it is being helped, and that should be enough for now, for it to trust and allow itself to be taken away;

- *The spirit feels sleepy*, either spontaneously or induced by the good spirits in order to more easily carry it to a suitable place on the unseen plane.

Upon noticing the spirit's "sleepiness," we can help by suggesting to such spirit that it rests peacefully and that, when it wakes up, it will continue to receive the help it needs.

2. The spirit does not yet know it has disincarnated, but is in condition to understand it?

Then, we should gear the subject to the theme of immortality. No need to talk about death, it suffices to talk about spiritual survival. If necessary, we can invite the spirit to make observations about the changes in itself and the ambience. When the spirit is already in a condition to understand them, short comments like those are enough for it to become aware of its situation.

If the spirit thinks that the dialoguer is together with it, in the same ambience and situation in which such spirit stands?

We should not worry about this detail, and not try to make the spirit understand that it is not so, that we are actually in a room, etc; for at that moment what matters is to attend to the spirit. Keep talking to it, trying to understand what its difficulty is and what to do to help it.

When it has understood its situation and does not need us anymore?

Then we can entrust it to the spirit rescuers, encouraging it to accompany them or be carried away by them.

3. The spirit knew it had disincarnated or learned just now, but still needs to accept situations or make inner changes?

We should help it settle into a more positive attitude, of a possible solution and of wanting to do something to solve its situation.

a) Help it understand why it came to be in such a situation of suffering;

b) Highlight the correctness and justice of the divine laws and the need for humility and forgiveness for the spirit to regain its balance and spiritually release itself;

c) Give legitimate hope: *All can be solved within the divine laws. God does not condemn us. He always forgives and loves us. You may do good to make up for the evil you committed.*

To conclude a dialogue with the suffering and perturbed, we may also say, as appropriate:

– *Thank God for the help you were given.*
– *Keep on striving to do right and improve yourself.*

– Take heart, because everything will be all right.
– Please go with the rescuers. Or: *Let them carry you away.*
– Maybe you can manifest yourself among us again, if you wish and if the spirit mentors allow it.

How much patience should we have in our language for addressing a perturbed and anguished spirit?

Imagine a man walking unconcernedly down a road. Suddenly, he unexpectedly has a syncope or is victim of an attack. He loses consciousness.

When he recovers his senses, how long will he need to collect his ideas? Everything seems confusing to him. It all seems strange. When we ask him who he is, of what family, where he lives, only with much difficulty will we get the answers and, sometimes, he does not even know his name.

As the inhabitants of the world beyond themselves say, such is the condition of a newly disincarnated spirit.

In unutterable anguish, they roam in space, imagining themselves to be alive, unaware of their new condition.

It is therefore necessary that the indoctrinators (dialoguers) should know how to speak to invisible fellow beings.

Aurélio A. Valente
(Practical and Doctrinal Spiritist Seances)

Let us understand each suffering spirit as if it were a nearest and dearest of kin, and then we will find the inner door through which we will talk to its heart.

7
Obsessors

Obsession is the process by which evil spirits knowingly and willingly harass incarnate (or other disincarnate) spirits, while trying to exert an insistent, dominant action on them, which is harmful.

They do that for various reasons.

For revenge

These are spirits which want to make suffer those who have hurt either them personally or their loved ones, during this or another incarnation.

To take advantage of some situation through the obsessed

Spirits attached to material sensations, want to enjoy them through the incarnate, besieging them for that. Leveraging or encouraging the tendencies that the incarnate may have, they lead him or her to acts which allow them to enjoy, through them, pleasurable sensations for which they no longer have the physical means.

Due to a deep and unbalancing connection with the obsessed

It is a connection which began in this lifetime or comes from earlier incarnations: a sickly infatuation; a pact made between the two; one's dominance and the other's dependence.

We even had a case in which the spirit wanted the obsessed to return to the religious group they both used to belong to.

For being an adversary of good

These sometimes do not have a personal relationship with their victims, but nevertheless attack a person or group for being at the service of good.

The divine law allows such harassment because it will serve to test a servant of the good; if the latter perseveres faithfully, the obsessor will be driven away or give up its purpose, or may even be attracted to the ideal of good, as demonstrated by the harassed.

Obsessor phalanxes

In a broader and more encompassing way, Hermínio C. Miranda, in his book *Diálogo com as Sombras* (*Dialogue with the Shadows*), examines the activity of these evil and lower-order spirits which organize themselves into phalanxes for revenge and domination over the incarnate and disincarnate; and identifies some of their members:

Darkness directors: These are spirits accustomed to action and command, therefore they have no patience for dialogue. They demand, order, threaten and intimidate.

And it should be added that this kind of spirit only communicates when it sees its subordinates being gathered by good spirits. Then it comes to "demand satisfaction" and tries to intimidate us.

Plotters: They do not feel directly responsible for what the phalanx does because they claim they "only plot it," they do not give orders.

But they are responsible too because, without them, darkness would have no coordination.

Jurists: These also state that they "only" examine the process of the victims and sentence them according to what is provided for in the codes of the "phalanx." They even think that they are distributing justice... But they too have their share of responsibility.

Executors: These, by their turn, do not feel responsible because they "only" execute it. It is not them that make any decisions. Yet they are responsible too because they accept being an instrument for evil.

Avengers: Spirits that do not rely on divine justice. They either ignore it or do not have the patience to wait for it; deem it too slow, and have taken the instruments of divine justice into their own hands, forgetting that we all make mistakes and have an obligation to forgive to be forgiven.

These shall be answerable for their wickedness and cruelty.

Religious: They present themselves as zealous workers of Christ, committed to the defense of "their" church. But what they do is defend their position of command, prominence and privileges, which they once had in the corporeal world and now want to continue to hold in the spiritual world.

Some of these are mere fanatics. They are also deluded by the power of suggestion of the obsessor phalanx.

They all will have to adjust themselves to the divine laws, by answering for their excesses and restarting their walk to progress.

Obsessors' minions

Many other spirits act at the behest of obsessor spirits of the phalanx because:

- They have been enslaved and do not know to react;
- Or they get something in return for what they do;
- Or they enjoy the evil they do (even without anything personal against the victim);
- Or out of sheer envy for those who are well.

Like all of us, they will answer for the evil they have done, but they will also receive encouragement and help to reform themselves.

Magnetizers and hypnotists

Hermínio C. Miranda also identifies a certain class of obsessors calling themselves wizards and sorcerers, which employ special techniques and resources of suggestion and influence, and of impregnation of objects and substances.

The effects they may cause are always the result of thought and will acting upon fluids; and conversely it will be our thought and will focused on goodness that will enable us to avert those effects or overcome them.

How they actually are

Spirit obsessors come with grudges, shouts, challenges, violence, aggressiveness...

However, they are nothing but unhappy beings, despite everything they say or do.

They want love (which is buried in their soul among hopes and disillusionments suffered) and defend themselves with an armor of hate, aggressiveness and hardness of feeling.

No matter if they treat us badly, or hurt us, but rather the impression or memory that we can leave in their hearts. Therefore, let us strive to make dialogue with them with human respect and brotherly affection as a keynote.

Deep down, they want to be convinced of their errors, to resume the evolutionary path which they abandoned long ago. Some are afraid to face the consequences of the evil they have done; others believe there is no possibility for them to be forgiven and be able to start over again.

But we Spiritists know that the divine providence has infinite and merciful ways and means for all of them to recover and resume the path of intellectual and moral progress. So let us not be disheartened nor discouraged in the reeducating process which is the dialogue with so-called spirit obsessors.

8

DISOBSESSION DIALOGUE

An obsession is a distressing and unhappy situation which Jesus and his apostles, according to the Gospel, were able to break by driving obsessors away and releasing the obsessed.

Following that sublime Master of spirituality, we also seek to rescue and support both victims and perpetrators caught in the meshes of obsession.

Healing passes and other magnetic resources disperse pernicious fluids with which the obsessed is surrounded and impregnated. But this is not always enough for him or her to be released from their obsessor.

May we not also combat the influence of evil spirits by moralizing them?

Yes; people too often fail to attempt this, but it is exactly what they ought to do; for it is frequently a duty laid upon you, and one that should be kindly and religiously accomplished by you. Your influence may bring them to repentance, and thus hasten their advancement. (*The Mediums' Book*, Ch. XXIII, Obsession, 254, 5)

To 'disobsess'[8] one must, as Kardec says, *act upon the intelligent being*. With *ably directed instructions*, the dialogue

---

8 [Trans. note] Same as "deobsess."

will enable us to give perverse spirits a *moral education,* i.e. to make repentance and a desire for good emerge in them, leading them to renounce their evil purposes.

Disobsession also requires some guidance to the obsessed incarnate, who need to change their thoughts and actions for the better, so as to not give rise to more actions by the obsessor. No obsession nor obsessor can resist when the beleaguered make sincere efforts for inner reform and devote themselves to good works.

By thus acting on both, the obsessor and the obsessed, we are assured by Kardec that *one can then have the sweet satisfaction of delivering an incarnate being and converting an imperfect spirit.*

How can a man possess in such cases more influence than is possessed by good spirits?

Perverse spirits are nearer to the human beings, to whom they come with the desire to torment them, than to the superior spirits, whom they do their utmost to avoid. When, in their approach to the former, they meet with those whose influence is calculated to make them better, they at first refuse to listen to them, and only laugh at their remonstrances; but if the human being persists judiciously in his effort to act upon them, they usually end by following his counsels. Elevated spirits are too far above them; they dazzle and terrify them by their splendor. Assuredly men have not more power than the higher spirits, but the influence of men is more consonant with their nature; and superior spirits, on seeing the ascendancy that a man may exercise over inferior spirits, recognize still more clearly the solidarity which exists between heaven and earth. (*The Mediums' Book*, 254, 5)

In fact, anyone working in mediumistic exchange, end up realizing that some spirits can understand us, incarnate souls, but have difficulty understanding higher order spirits, because they are not able to reach the mental frequency in which the latter communicate, nor do they understand the language of higher morality.

The issue of moral authority

Some people think that it would suffice to invoke the name of God to make evil spirits submit to them. St. Louis of France explains:

> The name of God has no influence over imperfect spirits, unless pronounced by someone whose own excellence enables him to use it with authority; in the mouth of one who has no moral superiority over the spirit, it is only a word, like any other. The most formidable weapon is inoffensive in the hands of those who have not the skill and the strength to use it. (*The Mediums' Book*, 279)

Let us go back to already mentioned Item 254:

> A man's ascendancy over spirits is always in proportion to his moral superiority. He can have no mastery over superior spirits, nor over those who, without having arrived at that grade, are good and kind but he can master all spirits who are inferior to himself in moral advancement.

That is why, although still imperfect, if we are willing to give brotherly help to our fellow beings, we have moral ascendancy over spirits that still remain in lower orders (either because they do not seek goodness yet, or still desire evil), and can talk to them in the work of disobsession, trying to enlighten them and dissuade them from exercising their evil actions.

Admirable medium Yvonne A. Pereira, in her book *A Luz do Consolador* (*By the Light of the Comforter*), narrates some edifying episodes in which she held brotherly dialogues with spirit obsessors, having managed to dissuade them from their purposes, and guide them to recommence in the spiritual life. In doing so, she says that of those former obsessors, now reformed spirits, she made many friends in bonds of esteem and confidence.

When talking to obsessors, keep the following in mind:

1. The obsessor should not be forcibly pulled out nor expelled; what are the reasons for their anger or hate? The incarnate may not be entirely a victim, owing to events in an previous life as well as his or her conduct in the current one.

2. Harshness, authoritarianism, sternness will not help our understanding with the obsessor. To touch them and gain their trust, our language must be sincerely brotherly; with a friendly warning and, when necessary, some energy; but generally speaking, filled with comfort, encouragement, and consolation.

Let us try to get them out of their fixed idea of revenge, hatred and destruction. Let us show them that we are interested that they will not later suffer the consequences of their wrongdoings.

Let us show them that the divine law takes care of teaching and correcting us and those who harm us, so there is no need for them to turn into avengers.

We should explain to them that the longer it takes for them to decide to improve themselves, the more difficult and laborious their own recovery will be.

If an obsessor threatens and challenges us

We should not be afraid. Let us be fearless, yet not reckless (precipitate, risky).

Let us not accept intimidation, for we will be afflicted only by what is within our spiritual debts, which we need for our progress. But we should not give it back with words or gestures of defiance or provocation. We should not ridicule a spirit's bravado nor defy its threats. To a spirit's sarcasm, let us not respond with derision.

In short, do not be intimidated, but be prudent. Because such spirits could often defeat us alone, individually; and it is only the protection provided by the spirit mentors' team that gives us support and momentary ascendancy over them.

If spirits accuse us of being worse than them and point out our faults

Be prepared for such situations with humility. As a spirit it watches us and may get informed about our failures, both current or in the past. And we are not redeemed spirits, whereas they are reprobates entangled in their crimes. Also it is no use trying to exhibit virtues we do no yet possess.

However, correct judgment will come through our efforts and not by already obtained results.

If we have patience and tolerance, such spirits will eventually admit that, even having not yet reached the higher stages of evolution, we are people who really want to be true Christians and friends, that our intentions are legitimate, our endeavored efforts are dignified; and they will respect us for that.

If a spirit argues with and shouts at us

Refrain from trying to beat such spirits in an argument. Sometimes, they are even better prepared for it than ourselves. And they always want to drag us into sour and violent arguments, for an atmosphere which befits their own agenda.

We, however, enlightened by Spiritism and as dialoguers, must discipline our emotions and feelings.

Direct the conversation to what really matters

Such spirits try to deceive and deny, not willing to enter their personal sphere, as it might reveal the fulcrum, the center of their problem. Without forcing it, we should try to gear the conversation towards that sphere.

If a spirit proposes an agreement, pact or bargain

We should simply refuse it without any indignation, aggressiveness or accusation. We may suggest that such spirit talks to our superiors, spirit mentors of our mediumistic work, for a decision; to which it will usually retort with: *But they are like you...* meaning they will not agree to it either.

Do not try to "trick" spirits with proposals or promises. While such spirits may try to deceive us, because they are disturbed and unbalanced, we on the contrary are not, and therefore must adopt better ways of relating and conducting ourselves.

If a spirit tries to keep talking nonstop

A spirit acts this way when it wants to escape listening to us, because, should it listen, it could be influenced for the good. While speaking, such spirit wants to influence us for evil, trying to shake our confidence and discourage us.

Let us insist, by making ourselves listened to with firmness, logic and love, and we will probably prevail over them.

If a spirit tries to involve other members of the group

Do not let it attract the whole group's attention to the conversation (through questions, gestures, jests, making them laugh, etc.), nor let it magnetically involve people (to make them emotionally moved). Warn participants about it.

As can we see, in the light of Spiritist knowledge, a dialogue which enlightens, consoles, warns, guides and encourages, is a precious resource for the task of disobsession.

And to think that some unwary fellow Spiritists have been recommending methods for disobsession in which counseling dialogues are not used!...

Spiritism has already placed in our hands such an enlightening knowledge, also showing us this excellent way! How could we possibly stop using the brotherly dialogue of light for the task of disobsession?

9

PRETOS-VELHOS, INDIANS AND CABOCLOS

In Brazil, in many seances, whether Spiritist or otherwise, there are often communications of spirits using specific language and traits, which are usually attributed to the figure of pretos-velhos,[9] Indians[10] and caboclos.[11]

However, once disincarnated, i.e. having no longer a physical body, a spirit no longer belongs to any of the earthly human ethnic groups; though they may present some of those features in their spiritual body (perispirit), if they still feel, or mentally conceive themselves, as such.

And, in order to communicate, all spirits basically employ the language of thought, without needing any peculiar language alien to the meeting participants.

Incidentally, scholars of African and Brazilian indigenous cultures, after analyzing the language used by such spirits when communicating in mediumistic meetings, have clarified the following:

1. The speech of pretos-velhos does not usually match the African dialects, even taking into account their blending with the Portuguese language. It is rather

9 The alleged spirits of old male and female Afro-Brazilian slaves.

10 Alleged spirits of Brazil's Native Americans.

11 Alleged spirits of Brazilians of mixed white and Native American or Native American and black ancestry.

some sort of gibberish without any meaning or connection with the way Africans used to speak.

2. A Brazilian Indian could not possibly have been
called Caboclo Sete Flechas (Caboclo of the Seven
Arrows), since their notion of numbers was limited
to the fingers of one hand.[12]

**Then why are there so many spirits presenting them
selves this way, in Brazil?**

Here are some possible reasons:

1. Pretos-velhos, Indians and caboclos are cherished
figures in Brazil's popular culture, and Umbanda[13]
has further encouraged belief in them.

2. Many people assume pretos-velhos, Indians and caboclos to be their inferiors, still remaining in a servant capacity to grant their requests. Others believe
that they have mysterious powers, capable of solv-
ing the consultants' problems in a magical way. And
perhaps people consider them venal, for accepting
to act in exchange for some "pay," some reward.

3. Evocations through specific rituals invite and
condition spirits to present themselves as pretos-
velhos, Indians or caboclos. And, many times, benevolent spirits will take on that appearance when

---

12 FRAGOSO, Sylvio Ourique, in "Mediunismo e Antroponomia"
["Mediumism and Anthroponomy"], *Revista Internacional de Espir-
itismo*, September 1981.

13 A syncretizing Brazilian religion with elements of African cults,
Roman Catholicism, and South American Indian practices.

manifesting themselves, for knowing that people will thus more easily accept their presence and message in their milieu.

Should we welcome them or not?

We must certainly give all communicating spirits a brotherly welcome, without any prejudice or intolerance. However, we should examine the nature and content of their communications, as we ought to do regarding any spirit that manifests itself among us.

1. If a spirit momentarily adopts that appearance or language because it was known as such during its earthly existence, and thus wants to prove its individuality?

   Such communication would then be justified, provided there was someone who could recognize and identify it, which is difficult now due to the very long time elapsed since slavery was abolished in Brazil.

2. If the spirit presents itself that way because it still feels in the same conditions as during its last incarnation?

   We must seek to help it release itself from that undesirable conditioning:

   – By enlightening it as to its real nature as a spirit;

   – By reminding it that it has had many other existences before, in different conditions, and therefore has a broader spiritual heritage;

   – By showing that there is no need for such fixation on the conditions of a previous, now ended existence; and that, in the spiritual life, it can continue progressing (even in its way of speaking).

3. If a spirit claims to present itself like that out of gratefulness to such incarnation, for having enabled it to acquire certain virtues, especially humility (through suffering unrighteous dominion without rebellion or hatred), which now it wants to exemplify?

We should tell it that we understand its purposes, but that humility does not consist in outward appearances nor servile attitudes; being humble is to not consider oneself better, or more deserving, than the others, to never place oneself above anyone.

4. If a spirit feigns such an appearance and language with the intent of deluding and disturb us?

Admonish it, warn it about its responsibility for its acts. If it disregards this, be firm for it to move away; ask for support from the spirit mentors, if necessary.

May legitimate pretos-velhos be spiritual guides?

Yes, if by word and deed they prove worthy of such title; if they have superior knowledge to guide us and true love to exemplify to us.

No, if they show little spiritual evolution and are still much attached to material sensations (such as smoking and drinking, for example).

Note: Most communications by pretos-velhos as spiritual guides are merely the result of suggestion and animism,[14] frauds and deceptions.

Surely there were good spirits which incarnated among slaves to lead those suffering people in a wise and loving way, during their captivity in Brazil.

Some of them, after disincarnating, may perhaps have been able to return to the earthly rearguard, out of love for those left behind, and also to continue their own spiritual growth in the service of good.

But there cannot have been many returning ones; on the contrary, these must have been very few. Because most African slaves were just like us: spirits of median or little evolution.

Was it possible that the latter – torn from their countries and homes, deprived of freedom, cruelly and mercilessly battered for years on end – were able to resign themselves and overcome their feelings towards their masters and executioners?

Very few spirits have triumphed in so hard a test, although all were given the opportunity of some intellectual and moral improvement in their trials and expiations.

Nevertheless, there are countless spirits of alleged pretos-velhos giving communications and professing to be spiritual guides of humanity, without the conditions for doing so.

---

14 In Spiritism, *animism* refers to any communication given by a medium's own incarnate soul rather than by a disincarnate spirit.

Conclusion

Spiritists warmly welcome, with all respect and brother-liness, manifestations of pretos-velhos, Indians and cabo-clos, as well as any other spirits allowed by God to come and have mediumistic exchanges with us (Eskimos or Inu-it, Arabs, Hindus, etc.).

But we do not abdicate our duty to analyze their com-munications in the light of Spiritism, because a Spiritist mediumistic exchange should be held according to high-er guidelines of truth and love, in order to give, or receive from, each communicant the spiritual enlightenment or help that it needs or can provide us with.

If we stop offering the usual conditioning which oc-curs in many mediumistic meetings held in Brazil, many spirits will cease presenting themselves as pretos-velhos, Indians or caboclos, and start communicating simply as spiritual beings, children of God.

(This topic is a modified version of "Chapter 20" from my book *Mediumistic Meetings: A Spiritist View*, Campi-nas, SP: Ed. Allan Kardec, 2016.)

10

ENDING THE COMMUNICATION

You have held a dialogue in the best possible way within your powers

Depending on the case, you have...

• calmed the distressed and agitated spirit;

• listened with brotherly interest to what it had to say;

• sought to understand its background or necessity;

• reasoned with the idea of immortality;

• explained the need to meet the laws of God;

• talked about hope through divine goodness;

• ensured the support and protection of good spirits;

• prayed with or for the communicating spirit.

You did so by using what you knew to the best of your capacity. And the communicating spirit received your assistance, according to its own disposition and free will, making good use, or not, of such conversation.

After that, the communicating spirit voluntarily moved away; or was carried away by the spirit mentors; or went with the spirit rescuers.

What should you do when a spirit...

a) refuses to speak or does not show any signs of making good use of the enlightenment or vibrations it has just received?

b) takes too long to withdraw itself due to some indecision or a desire to stay beyond the allotted time?

You should do as follows:

1. Explain to the spirit, in a brotherly way, the damage that such an attitude is causing to the medium (fluidic wear, painful impressions, etc.) and to the meeting's progress (other spirits still await to be attended to); then ask the spirit to leave.

   If it happens at the end of the meeting, inform it:

   Our time is up, so we must stop at this point;

   To the undecided, you may suggest:

   Go with the spirit rescuers.

   Inform those being moved away:

   If permitted by the spirit mentors, you'll return another time and then we will talk better.

2. If the spirit dismisses your request, fix your thoughts on the good, and order it to leave.

   It is customary to say:

   Depart, in the name of God (or *in the name of Jesus*).

If you think it necessary, before ordering the spirit to leave, ask for help from the other participants of the group (that they concentrate their thoughts and stay in silent prayer).

You may also ask the medium to break concentration, thus interrupting the communication and returning to his or her normal state.

Dispersive passes, for decreasing the amount of fluids, may also promote the breaking of the trance.

3. If the spirit remains opposed and does not withdraw, pray fervently, asking for the interference of the spirit mentors, which will certainly not fail to come and help you efficiently and decisively.

At the end of communications, you should do as follows:

- To the spirit mentors: Thank them for their presence and assistance;

- To the spirit friends: Greet them goodbye;

- Help the mediums to awake and recompose themselves, if necessary.

A dialoguer's prayer

Lord! To the task of attending to needy spirits, I present myself.

I know that in my heart I hold no perfection of human feelings, but I have been striving to attain it, struggling for my inner reform.

While developing this role, I will always be discreet, never exposing unnecessarily the personal dramas of communicating spirits.

At this valued moment, I shall act as an intermediary of your teachings.

May my effort in the Good make me worthy of spiritual help, through intuitions.

And if, for some reason, those attended to by me do not feel touched, I shall ask you in prayer: *Forgive my flaws and receive those spirits in your mercy.*

I will never argue with spirits, on the pretext of showing scholarship or superiority.

I will guard against defiance, while guiding and respecting those fellow beings stuck to ideas of anger or revenge.

Your Gospel will be my shield, your love will be turned into a defense weapon, and charity will always be my companion in the struggle for the spiritualization of humanity.

I will not fear, for my seriousness of purpose and willingness to do good will attract spiritual protection.

May I develop patience and common sense in order to better serve.

I will study the Spiritist teachings as much I can, so that the proper words and guidance do not fail me when I am making the dialogue.

When vigorous action is called for to curb excesses, please sustain me so that discipline does not turn into irritation.

Compassion and goodness will always be my work goals.

I will not cultivate vices. I will get rid of evil-speaking and strive to suppress my evil tendencies, thus gaining moral authority.

And above all, Master Jesus, help me make such dialogue with my own conscience, when my own imperfections resemble those of unbalanced spirits, so that I testify in my inner self to what I verbalize in the meetings.

Lord, hear my prayer and sustain me while I attend to the needy, so that the dialogue is turned into an instrument of spiritual liberation and redemption.[15]

15 Spirit Nora (Message channeled by Emanuel Cristiano, during a meeting held on 03/20/1998, at CEAK, Campinas – SP, Brazil).

PART THREE
EXAMPLES AND CASE STUDIES

1
ABOUT THE EXAMPLES OFFERED HEREIN

We must reiterate that our objective, when talking to spirits in mediumistic meetings, is not one of merely studying the communicating spirits, but rather the Christian purpose of consoling, rebuilding morale, enlightening and guiding the spirits which more constantly manifest themselves in such meetings: those in need of help or guidance.

This book's objective is to help prepare anyone who wishes to collaborate in attending to communicating spirits in mediumistic meetings.

But do not think that the examples being offered are sufficient for someone to become an expert dialoguer, for they represent only a small sample of a variety of cases and situations which may arise in mediumistic meetings.

Hopefully, it will give interested parties an idea about the nature and state of communicating spirits when they come to mediumistic meetings in a Spiritist center, and how we can engage in fruitful dialogue with them, if we want to help them in a brotherly way.

To record in writing the entire content of each dialogue held with needy spirits would have required many more pages, making it impossible to present the necessary minimum number of examples.

Only some cases were transcribed in their entirety, such as: A spirit which felt extremely hurt and therefore turned rebellious and aggressive; another one which acted under the command of malevolent spirits; and one which claimed to have committed suicide "for love."

As to the other dialogues, only the most interesting or expressive extracts of each of them were chosen to be shared with the reader.

In these extracts we see the most common reasons for the actions of communicating spirits, and the main argumentations we may use to enlighten them and invite them to renew their attitudes.

A highlight in this collection of dialogues is the case of "A proven identity," in which the opportunity is taken to clarify how we learned over the years, in the services held at Centro Espírita Allan Kardec, in Brazil, that the main objective of communicating with spirits lies not in personal messages or family news (which would require a perfect identification of the communicating spirits), but rather in attending to anonymous spirits, our fellow beings regardless, sent to us by Heaven for reception and assistance.

The examples herein presented to the reader's consideration were all collected in mediumistic meetings at our Spiritist center.

Apart from cases obtained through my own experience, I have also made use of the work of many anonymous and devoted dialoguers of our Spiritist center – may God's blessings come to them all.

One of those is Henri B. F. Barreto whom I thank for reporting two cases attended to by him, which I took the opportunity to comment on and are now entitled "This is not my body" and "In the anatomical theater."

For providing a valuable contribution, special mention goes to Ana Maria Checchinato, who has been recording many examples of dialogues, and each year teaches our center's "Course for Dialoguers," essential for preparing new workers for this meritorious occupation.

2

NOT SUFFERING, BUT BEREFT OF SOMETHING...

A devout woman adrift

I noted her presence through the medium's demonstration of being involved by a spirit, and went on to attend to her. To our initial greeting, she replied:

"I'm fine."

What brought you here?

"I really enjoy going where people are praying, as you do here."

Indeed, we've learned to pray from Jesus, raising our thoughts to God, our Father.

"When I was on Earth..."

So, you know that you're on the spiritual plane?

"Yes, and I really enjoyed leaving life on Earth, because now I can go where there's singing and praying to God."

You couldn't before?

"No. I was born and raised in the farm countryside. Hard work with almost no amusements... I wanted to go to church, but it was far away and we had to work... Only every once in a while, once in a blue moon, I could go to church.

It was so beautiful! I enjoyed it so much!... Then marriage came in, with husband and small children. It became ever more difficult to go to any church... In came the grandchildren and I had to help raise them... Then one day, I died! Freedom! Now I can go anywhere I want. I'm fine."

(I understood that she had led a life of honesty, service, and dedication to her family, and was not tied to past problems. What to do, leave her like that? Certainly not. She lacked in better guidance for the spiritual life, having limited herself to wandering on the earthly plane. Then I asked her:)

Did you know that, on the life plane where you are now, there are places where you can learn about God, his laws, and how to serve Him?

"Really?! I haven't seen any yet..."

If you wish, you can go visit them. They also pray and sing there, but they do more, they tell about all things that Jesus has taught us, and what we should do to also be one of his disciples, helping other people.

"Be a disciple of Jesus?... I wish I could!..."

I'll ask one of these spirit friends to take you to visit one of those places where we learn how to love God and neighbor. Is any of them already next to you?

Naturally there was one, because the spirit friends were just waiting for her to be awakened to the possibility of a better guidance in the afterlife, to introduce themselves to her. And, contented, there she went with them, the previously adrift, devout woman...

The atheist

If we think that not believing in God prevents a spirit from feeling reasonably well when disincarnate, we will be surprised with communications of some atheists, such as this one:

Welcome, in the name of God's love we greet you.

"I don't believe in God but I thank you for your welcome."

Do you know where you are?

"Well, since you speak of God, I guess this is some sort of religious meeting. I was just a boy when I distanced myself from religion. To me science and philosophy are my religion, everything in which I believe. With them I learned to be honest and supportive, for human beings are only as good as what they know and feel, and must have dignity..."

Congratulations on your attitude. Would that all humanity thought like that! In Spiritism, we also rely heavily on philosophy and science. Our philosophy, however, finds its culmination in the religious aspect.

"I can't see any mystical symbols or rituals here..."

To us, adoration should be done "in spirit and in truth" as taught by Jesus. It needs no outward displays but has to be very sincere and true inwardly.

"Interesting! I didn't know this philosophy. Spiritism, eh? What is it about?"

The origin, nature and destination of spirits, and their relation with the corporeal world.

"Corporeal world... I know I'm no longer in it because I saw when my body was buried... I've been going from place to place, to wherever some higher subject of study attracts my interest..."

(Due to his way of thinking and acting in life, he did not appear to be suffering in the spiritual world. What was he lacking?)

"But I'm getting a bit tired or bored, I don't know..."

It must be getting repetitive, mustn't it? However, life on the spiritual planes is as infinite as the universe. Planes which are invisible to human eyes, yet perfectly real.

What are you talking about?

About the places where live the spirit messengers which come to this meeting...

Are they spirits? To me, they look like people...

Indeed they are people just like you. The souls of men and women who lived down here on Earth and continue living and progressing in the hereafter.

"Interesting... I hadn't noticed this activity of theirs... I think I was only focused on what drew my attention. They're showing me some books now..."

They can exchange a lot of information with you and explain the destination of humanity through unceasing progress. If you wish, you can follow on with them.

"I really want to know it. I'm going to talk to them..."

We were left wondering what wondrous and happy discoveries were waiting for him on the plane of immortal life; an atheist whose life was already guided by honesty and brotherliness, as every good Christian's life should be.

3
Does a spirit really need that?

A spirit may think it is feeling hungry, thirsty, cold or hot, and manifest itself asking for food, drink, some cool relief or warm clothes; but actually, as it no longer possesses a physical body, it has no need for anything material.

Moved by the condition of a spirit which claims to be thirsty, and wanting to relieve it of that discomfort, less experienced dialoguers make the medium drink some water, thus believing that they are catering to the spirit's need. However the medium is not thirsty and the spirit, without a physical body, does not need it.

If we believed that, in similar cases, to relieve a spirit of sensations of hunger, thirst, cold or heat, we would have to make the medium drink some water, be dressed in warm clothes, and so on, then how would we cater to a spirit which had been an alcoholic and now wants some drink, or a spirit which was a drug addict and now desperately begs for some? Would we give the medium alcohol and drugs? Certainly not!

So, how to attend to a suffering spirit or one stuck in some vicious addiction? In such cases, we have had success taking the communicating spirit's attention away from the feeling it still believes to be suffering – the impression that remained from the moment its discarnation, similar to the withdrawal effects of the drug addiction – and assuring it, in a brotherly way, that rescue is already in progress and that such feeling will pass.

Here is one example:

You're already being relieved of that thirst. You no longer need to feel so thirsty, because God the Father who loves us all, loves you as well, and does not want you to keep suffering like that.

Did you know that this thirst you feel is not of the body? It's of the soul. To quench this thirst, Jesus offers living water. Do you want this living water, so you'll never be thirsty again?

After getting the spirit's interest, we should explain to it:

Just learn from Jesus that we are spiritual beings, that we never die and, as spirits, the thirst or hunger that we feel is of faith, of knowledge of the things of God, and of love and peace...

If the spirit has a feeling of cold, of being buried in a glacier for example, we may say:

You've been removed from there. It was really cold, wasn't it? But now you're in a safe and warm place. Feel the warmth... Doesn't it feel better now?

In a like manner, we can rescue a spirit which was an accident victim and still feels trapped in the wreck, under the rubble, or one that disincarnated during a fire or by drowning. We shall assure it that it was rescued and has managed to get out of that situation, and will now be taken care of and assisted.

Rarely do we tell a spirit in such a condition: *You have died there, in that accident or situation,* because it may not be emotionally or spiritually prepared to accept the fact calmly, nor understand it, and then will enter into despair, hindering the task of a helping dialogue. To tell a spirit that it has disincarnated, it is necessary that the spirit itself have noticed what happened and mentions it, in which case we should comfort it with the support it is being given and the assurance of immortality.

To a drug or alcohol addict, besides suggesting that it is being soothed, we may open up a field of new interest to it by saying:

No, we can't give you that because it would harm instead of helping you. You are addicted to it because you don't yet know that there is another "drink" (or "substance") which has an even more pleasant effect and causes you no harm... Interested? Then those spirit friends which are there can show you how it is. Can you see them? They know how we may get inebriated with the good, with love of life and neighbor, and find joys of the soul, pure joys, which will harm neither us nor the others, and make us feel very, very good!

In such cases, it is not just because we are talking to it and using some beneficial suggestion that a spirit will experience some improvement in its condition. It will be because the spirit friends, availing themselves of our guiding of the communicating spirit's thoughts (a guiding which at times they themselves inspired), make use of special procedures in the fluidic field, acting on its perispirit to relieve the spirit and promote balance recovery.

And such attending to the spirit is only an emergency one, because rescue for the communicating spirit will be carried on in the hereafter, in special colonies providing support and treatment for this kind of suffering spirits. We will however have helped these fellow beings with a first contact to raise awareness of the reality of their spiritual condition.

4

"THIS IS NOT MY BODY"

It is very common during mediumistic seances, that spirits which disincarnated as victims of violent deaths, murders or accidents, addiction or suicide, manifest themselves.

Many of them do not believe they are dead and claim emphatically to be alive.

Let us look at a communication of one such sufferer, which did not accept his own death.

"Untie me because I must get back at Chico," he affirmed with insistence.

Why do you want to get back at him?

"He's shot me and hurt me for real."

(It seemed to have been a summary execution, and by the way he spoke, he gave me the impression of still being close to his body.) Then I suggested:

Whose body is that close by?

"I don't know, it's lying face down..."

Take a good look, examine it.

"He's wearing a shirt of this soccer team and has a tattoo. I also have a tattoo just like that... But many fans of that team wear the same shirt and have the same tattoo."

(Despite noting the evidence, the spirit would not admit to itself that the body it was seeing was its own.)

Let's take a look at his face, do you recognize it?

"It looks like me but it can't be me, because I'm here alive and well."

(I avoided insisting on that, but was inspired to ask.)

Are you noticing the approach of someone?

"Yes, a late uncle of mine..."

Would you like to follow on with him?

Still insecure, he replied:

"Yes..."

And there he went, together with his also disincarnate relative who would certainly explain everything to him later on.

But not every spirit that has disincarnated of a violent death experiences this illusion of still be living in a body. What would contribute to this?

Kardec asked if the knowledge of Spiritism could exert some influence on the longer or shorter duration of a spirit's disturbance after its death, to which the spirit instructors replied:

"It exercises a very considerable influence on that duration, because it enables the spirit to understand beforehand the new situation in which it is about to find itself ; but the practice of rectitude during the earthly life, and a clear conscience, are the conditions which conduce most powerfully to shorten it." (*The Spirits' Book*, question 165)

In that same question, the spirit instructors clarify that the disturbance duration may be a few hours or even many years.

Thus we learn that, for knowing Spiritism, a spirit may more quickly understand that it has disincarnated.

But it is not the mere knowledge of Spiritism that will ensure a good situation or a happy reception in the spiritual world, but rather the worthiness the spirit may have, by virtue of having done good in earthly life and being of a clear and peaceful conscience.

Hence the difference between a spirit soon realizing that it has disincarnated and others taking longer to understand and accept their new condition. But every one of them will sooner or later understand their spiritual state and, by the mercies of God, continue living and progressing.

5
MOTHER OF SMALL CHILDREN

She presented herself in an anguished state and with a fixed idea:

"My children, my children! I can't leave them, what will become of them without me? I've got to go back..."

Note: This is usually one of the most difficult cases for dialoguers, due to the emotional burden involved. Who would not be moved by this mother's situation? And it is also difficult because the mother is focused on her desire to return, barely listening to what the dialoguer says.

(The dialoguer sought a "gap" in the monologue of the grieving mother while saying words of comfort and hope:)

Please calm down, we understand your concern, but your children are getting support, everything is going to work out, trust in God!

(But since the communicating spirit persisted in distress, the dialoguer used another approach, speaking a little more incisively:)

Do you really want your children to receive some help? If you do, please listen to what I have to say to you. Otherwise you'll stay there grieving and achieve nothing good. So now, will you let me speak?

"Can you really help me?"

For sure. You were brought here to receive support. God is love, He knows everything we're going through and what we need. These spirit friends have come here to help you... Can you see them?

"Not very well. It seems like they're around and talking to me, but I don't want to know, I only want to come back and be with my children again."

(In view of her reply, we noticed that conditions existed for her to be helped, but she was unwilling to accept anything but what she wanted.)

Well, you need to understand that we can't fight the laws of God, nor want to change what's already happened...

"But it has to change, it has to change, I've got to go back!..."

Please calm down, we can't change the divine laws, but there are other resources and help within these laws for us to solve the situation in the best possible way

"But how, how? I'm dead already!"

Only your body has died. You go on living spiritually and, in this spiritual life, there's the continuance of affections; other situations arise for coexistence, learning, and serving. Life goes on...

"Will you stay with me and help me?"

It's these spirit friends that will stay with you and help you. They're better able to support and guide you, because they're on the same plane as you. They'll show you that just as you are receiving help, your children are also being supported; you'll have the opportunity of seeing your children and talking to them again.

"Is this possible? I want it, I want it..."

You'll have to be calm and well prepared for this re-union. For that reason, they're going to take you for rest and treatment, and to enlighten you about the continuity of life in the environment where you are now...

"All this takes time..."

Not too long and it'll be worth it; later on you'll see your children again.

"Oh, my God, let me see my children!"

For sure, God will let you see them again, for He doesn't keep us forever apart from those we love and his laws always seek our good, even if at the moment we can't understand them.

"They're calling me..."

Please accede and go with them, these spirit friends, it's for your own good. Trust and keep the hope of reuniting with your children, when God allows it.

"When God allows it. Yes, yes..."

6

WHEN A SPIRIT FEELS LIKE A CHILD

When disincarnating, a spirit which animated a child usually finds prompt help and proper ambience in the hereafter.

If facing problems with the divine laws, such spirit may at first find some difficulties, but then help for overcoming them will not fail it.

Also, at times the spirit's perispirit maintains an infantile appearance because it will soon be reincarnating.

Some of these "child" spirits are allowed to come to our mediumistic meetings to receive the help they need and for us to get acquainted with that reality of spiritual life.

Therefore, now and then we will have to make dialogue with spirits which disincarnated when their bodies were still in the first years of their earthly existence.

How will they speak to us, when communicating through mediums?

That is what Kardec asked the spirits (*The Mediums' Book*, item 282, 35):

How is it that the spirit of a little child can reply to us with full intelligence, when, on earth, he had not even arrived at self-consciousness?

To which the spirit instructors replied:

"The soul of an infant is *a spirit confined in the swaddling-clothes of matter*, but when disengaged from matter, he regains the use of his faculties as a spirit, for *age has no existence for spirits*. The fact that the spirit of an infant can answer you like that of an adult proves that he had lived before."

Because of this initial explanation, some people think that the spirit which animated a child should talk as an adult when communicating; but they failed to pay closer attention to the end of the Spirits' response:

"Nevertheless, until he is completely disengaged from matter, he may retain some traces of the characteristics of infancy."

So a child's spirit may speak to us as an adult, if it has already sufficiently restored itself on the spiritual plane, regaining full possession of all its intellectual powers.

However, it will talk to us in a childish manner and show the interests of a child, if it has not yet fully detached itself from the impressions of the physical body.

For that very reason, the dialogue with a spirit which feels like a child requires a special way which can meet the possibilities of understanding of the communicating spirit. One must also be on guard against spirits which appear to feel like a child but are actually faking it to deceive us. An alert dialoguer will notice such deception by the way the spirit holds a conversation, because it will let out here and there expressions and knowledge that a child could not possibly have, and thus attend to the deceiver without being fooled by it, also warning it of the responsibility for its conduct.

Now, let us recall one of those dialogues in which a spirit did actually feel like a child:

"I want my mom. Where is my mom? I was in the street and everything was gone, I can't find my home... I'm scared... Mom will be angry with me..."

No, no, she won't. We'll send word to her that you are here, till you can get back or she can come to see you.

"Who are you? My mom told me not to talk to strangers..."

With bad strangers, right? Because me, I only want to help you.

"I don't know..."

You think I'm bad?

"No, you don't seem bad."

And the others who are there?

(It is assumed that the spirit is able to see the spirit friends and, generally, that is what happens.)

"They also seem nice. Some are dressed in white. They are doctors? Is this a hospital here?"

No it isn't, but this is a place where people are helped. Here everyone seeks to love one another, like Jesus taught to us. Do you know who Jesus is?

"Mommy taught me to pray to baby Jesus..."

Really? That's good. How did she teach you?

"Baby Jesus take care of me so I can be a good boy. Take care of my dad and my mom too. Amen."

Now that's a beautiful prayer! Well done! That's why you arrived here, you're not going to be lost any more, and later your mom will come to see you.

"What a beautiful place!... There's a garden there... Lots of kids playing..."

You may go there to have some fun too, if you like. Would you like to?

"Yes, sure I want. There's this "aunt" here saying I can go with her."

(As a projection produced by the spirit friends, that spirit had begun to see the grounds of a spiritual colony for children, while a friendly female entity approached to help it.)

Yes, you can, she's nice too. May God go with you!

7
What does an angel look like?

"Hey, I'm Carol."

How are you, Carol?

"Very sad..."

Why? Please tell me...

"Teddy fell in a hole..."

Who's Teddy?

"It's my teddy bear. Can't you see it in the hole?"

How old are you?

"Five. And you?"

Well, I'm certainly older than you.

"And you came to help me get my Teddy? It's my dearest toy. I have no daddy and no mummy, can't be without Teddy. You pick it up for me?"

If you have no daddy nor mommy, who takes care of you?

"I live in a house with many girls and we have aunts that take care of us. You have children?"

Yes, I do.

"They're small?"

No, they're already quite big...

"Let's go pick up Teddy? I'm afraid to go near the hole. I'm afraid I can fall..."

(Then the small child's spirit started to cry.)

No need to cry, Carol. I'll ask our Father in Heaven to help us. Who knows? Maybe He sends someone to pick Teddy up. You know our Father of Heaven?

"No, I don't know, never saw him. I only know He's nice and lives up there in the clouds..."

Then let's ask, maybe He'll help us by sending a little angel to pick Teddy up, won't He?

"You're afraid of the big hole, aren't you, uncle?"

Let's ask then?

(Then the dialoguer made a prayer using simple words, asking our Father in Heaven to send some help for Carol's little friend.)

"Uncle, the little angel will really come?"

Let's wait for a bit...

"I can hear a noise, it's him?"

Let's check it calmly...

"Uncle!"

Yes? I can hear you...

"The little angel is coming to pick up Teddy!"

Oh, good! See? Our Father in Heaven is really "neat."

"Uncle?"

Yes?

"Oh! the little angel has no blonde hair and no curls... Uncle?"

I can hear you.

"He also has no wings, and his hair is black!..."

Never mind that. There are angels with many different hair colors, and they need no wings to fly.

"Uncle?!"

What's it now?

"I'm crying with joy... He got into the hole and picked up my Teddy!"

What a neat little angel! See? You you need not cry any more.

"Uncle, he's giving Teddy back to me. Hey, that's odd!?"

What's odd?

"The little angel is Japanese!"

How "cool," you see? Our Father in Heaven makes all sorts of little angels. What matters is you already got your Teddy back.

"Yes, uncle. Thanks. I liked you a lot. Don't you want to take me to your home?"

I'd love to, but I can't.

"Uncle, I'm happy to have my Teddy back and I'm going to play with these other kids that are coming now..."

Go, darling, may God go with you.

Throughout this counseling, the dialoguer had talked in a language within the reach of that spirit which still felt like a child, and focused on the motivation brought by the "little girl": to retrieve her toy.

In the spiritual colony where she was sent to, she would certainly be with spirits that would maintain their infantile appearance because they would soon be reincarnating. There are many such colonies in the spiritual world.

She believed in angels. Many believe in them too and think they are beings created apart from humanity as pure spirits, whereas we, human beings, would be flesh and soul.

Interesting indeed was the practical revelation that they move about by flying, without the need of wings, and have human appearance. That is because angels are good spirits, the souls of people who inhabited Earth and now, on the spiritual plane, watch over us in the name of God's love.

8

IN THE ANATOMICAL THEATER

A spirit came in complaining:

"This smell is too strong! Too strong... It's formaldehyde... I think it's formaldehyde... And those guys are lacking in respect for me. How come they can mess with my body like that?"

When attended to by a dialoguer, the spirit identified itself:

"I lived begging on the streets... You know what this means?"

(The dialoguer showed understanding, solidarity, and agreed with the spirit:)

A hard life for sure.

(He knew he had died. Nobody had claimed his body, which then was taken to the anatomical theater of a medical school, where it was being mercilessly dissected by students. What would that spirit have done to still feel connected to its physical body, even knowing that it was dead? Was it an attachment to material life even though it had been so miserable? Or a contempt for life, which had led to alcohol and drug abuse? We did not know!)

(Then the dialoguer sought for inspiration, which came as follows:)

My brother, life is the most precious gift that God has given us, his children. And life in the body is very valuable for our evolution.

"Valuable? Even a miserable life like mine?"

Whatever may be the condition of our existence, it is always valuable, because it gives rise to new experiences, serving and learning. It's by living that we spirits progress and become more experienced.

"I don't know what experience I got from my life..."

At the very least you've learned that it's better to lead a life of work, raise a family and take care of it, than to stay begging on the streets...

"Well, now, that's true. I'd have to fight hard for a living but at least I wouldn't have suffered as much as I did alone on the streets..."

You know that neglecting your body and indulging in vices is like committing suicide?

"But I didn't want to kill myself!"

It was unintentional but it was suicide all the same, because it shortened your life which could have lasted longer and been very useful to you and other people.

"I wasn't thinking..."

Maybe that explains why, despite having died, you still remain attached to your body. You weren't supposed to be dead yet...

"But they're slashing my body..."

Don't be sad about it. Your body is useful because those students, although seeming to slash it with no respect, are actually learning how the human body is and functions, and once they've learned it, they'll be able to save many lives later on. Besides, that was not your true body, but rather this one you have now is your spiritual body.

Such explanation reassured that suffering spirit which could then be entrusted to the brotherly care of spirit friends.

Rokitansky, an emeritus professor at the University of Vienna, author of several works on pathological anatomy, personally performed autopsies on many bodies during his long career, and watched his students doing autopsies on many others, perhaps thousands of bodies in total.

This great physician and researcher of the nineteenth century, besides his magnificent work, also had a great humanitarian sensibility.

As can be noticed in the following text of his:

Remember that this body was born from the love of two souls; it grew cradled by the faith and hope of the one who snuggled it in her womb; it smiled and dreamed the same dreams of children and young people; it certainly loved and was loved and longed for those who departed; it cherished one happy tomorrow and now lies on the cold slab, without a single tear shed for it, nor a single prayer said for it. Its name? God only knows. Yet an inexorable fate gave it the power and greatness of serving humanity, which passed by it indifferently.

9

AWAKENING TO THE TRUTH

"You have no authority to speak in the name of Jesus! Only the priests of our church can do it! How dare you?"

Sister, Jesus used to say to all those who became his disciples: *Go and preach!* We're only doing what Jesus commanded...

"That was for his disciples. You're not disciples of Jesus."

Why not? Jesus assured, *I have other sheep that are not of this fold,* and told his disciples to pass his message to others. So we also now are learning and teaching the Gospel of Jesus. Did you hear us say anything contrary to the teachings of the Master?

"I don't know... But you just can't, you can't!"

I think we can, sister, because we've been doing it and many have heard and answered the calls we have made in the name of Jesus. But that's not what matters right now. How are you? How do you feel?

"I'm fine... Nothing much..."

Do you know where you are?

"I've been walking here and there. I even feel a little tired now."

Then you've come to the right place. Here you'll be able to take a rest. It's a place of brotherly love, as taught by Jesus. You know that Jesus proved that life doesn't end when we die, don't you?

"Yes, with the resurrection..."

Exactly, when he appeared in spirit even after being crucified. And we learned from him that each one of us will resurrect as well. Isn't that good news?

"Why are you talking of death?..."

I'm not talking about death, but life immortal. The body doesn't last forever, the spirit however lives on.

"I'm very much alive..."

Spiritually, yes.

"In body and soul!"

Have you noticed the place where we are now? It's a room with several people in it...

"Some of them are helping others who seem to be ill..."

Those are the Lord's messengers rescuing the souls of those who arrive here without fully realizing that they're no longer living in the earthly world...

"Wait a minute, again you seem to be telling me that I've died. No way have I died."

Indeed, you haven't died. Only your body...

"My body?! This is my body, look...

(At that moment she paid attention to the body and saw it was not hers, for she was acting and speaking through a medium's body.)

"What's this? This is not my body! Witchcraft!..."

No, this is the work of God's mercy. He lets us talk through someone else, when we no longer have a body but need to talk. It's just like talking on a telephone.

"What a weird thing!... And now what? Will I stay here, inside this woman?"

No, this was only for you to realize that you're still living. Now, you'll be guided in the spiritual world with the help of these messengers of the Lord, which I talked to you about and that you can see.

"Alas, I'm not really understanding much. But I'm so tired..."

They will take care of you, take you to rest. Later, when you wake up, you'll get to know more. The hand of God is in all this, sustaining every one of us, as Jesus taught us. Stay confident, okay?

"All right... I trust in God..."

Then she fell asleep and was carried away by the spirit friends to later wake up a little more enlightened about her condition, under their support.

10
ATTENDING TO A PSYCHIATRIST

A dialoguer made the initial greeting welcoming the spirit which then asked:

"What am I doing here? What place is this?"

Something must have happened to your health, and for that reason you're in a "spiritual emergency room."

(The dialoguer was a beginner and did not know, or had forgotten, that one must speak like that to the communicating spirit.)[16]

Feeling very strongly upset, the spirit replied: "What emergency room? My health is excellent and nothing happened to me. I'm a doctor, what's with this 'spiritual emergency room' story?!"

(The dialoguer tried to argue in various ways, but unbalance in the communicating spirit's mind, as a result of her inappropriate initial statement, had already taken place, making it hard to talk to him.)

Then she asked for the assistance of a more experienced dialoguer, who said: Sorry for the "misunderstanding." Often we don't know how to deal properly with words.

---

16 Please check Part Two of this book, in "Starting the dialogue," what not to say.

Let me ask you, what's your specialty as a doctor? Because we have many patients in need of care here.

"In that case, I'm at your disposal, I'm a psychiatrist and would like to be of help."

We're happy to count on your help. Please talk with these other doctors who are there doing the screening of the sick.

"Now I see what happened...," said the communicating spirit, outlining a smile.

What are you talking about?

"The woman that came to talk to me before you belongs to the "unbalanced" group that I'll be able to help with treatment. Now I understand her mentioning a 'spiritual emergency.' Poor thing, I was very rude to her..."

(That was not quite what had happened but the spirit calmed down by thinking so.)

The fellow doctors await your help..., said the dialoguer.

"I'm ready, I'm going to talk to them."

And there he went to meet the spirit friends which, in a brotherly way, at the right moment and with adequate words, would make him understand his condition of a disincarnate spirit continuing to live in the hereafter.

11

LIKE A DIAMOND IN THE MUD

A spirit lamented after being made aware of its condition and of the necessity of improving itself:

"I'll have to forget this personality and calm down my mind. Because it's a torment..."

Don't forget you're a son of God...

"Me, a son of God?..." He said disheartened.

Yes, and we, God's children, are all as valuable as diamonds. Only sometimes we let ourselves fall into the mud and get covered with stains and excrescences, seemingly losing our spiritual shine...

"That's what happened to me, that's what happened to me..."

A day comes, however, when those stains and excrescences are removed little by little, and with our efforts we may shine again. Because God created us for this purpose, to shine. "*Let your light shine,*" said Jesus.

"But I'm darkness... I'm not able to love and so far only did evil."

We aren't darkness at all. Nobody is. We're all light, only such light is covered in dust, dipped in mud, blurred... And our job is to remove all that which is undue in us.

"How will I be able to do this, how?"

Trust! The good spirits which are helping you believe in you because they know you're a spirit child of God, full of potential as any of us. You have to overcome these barriers, find renewing experiences, and finally trust in yourself again.

"I've been crying a lot!... Recalling my childhood, my misdeeds..."

But you'll balance yourself again, find stability and a new life direction.

"Yes, there's no other option. Funny how you reach a point where there's no other way."

True, because our free will only goes so far...

"So many illusions, aren't there?"

... and when, in our free will, we reach a point where there are no more experiences or benefits to be had, then divine mercy begins to propel us up, to the top. This is what's happening to you now.

"Yes, up, to the top!..." He muttered, between sad and hopeful. And with this new frame of mind, that repentant sinner, with the help of the spirit friends, headed for his new opportunities of learning and repairing the evils he had committed, and for readjustment.

12
SHE WAS IN THE ICU...

It was a young woman who communicated saying that she was in an ICU. In despair, she said:

"Look, they turned off the machines! They're trying to kill me! I don't want to die, I'm young, got my whole life ahead of me..."

Then she asked:

"Was it you who turned them off? Why did you do that to me? Help! Call the doctors, quick!"

It was clear that the young woman had disincarnated but not realized or understood her new situation. She was no longer in the ICU, although she felt that way, and her physical death had not taken place because someone turned off the machines, but rather the machines were turned off because her body had died.

It was not convenient to tell her what had really happened then, for the dialoguer was not sure if she could take the news well.

The dialoguer then tried to calm her down:

We're going to call a doctor, for sure, and you'll be rescued. But you won't die, certainly not, nobody dies, we're children of God, immortal spirits...

(The dialoguer's intention was to open up an avenue to a higher order of thinking. The communicating spirit, however, had a fixed idea about being in danger and needing help.)

"I want my family. Where are they? I want to leave here and go home. Help me! Bring me a phone, I'll call my parents."

(And as the dialoguer was trying to propose a different angle, she cut it short.)

"Hurry up, where's that phone! Enough idle talk."

It then occurred to the dialoguer, perhaps by inspiration, to make the following observation:

Have you noticed that you're breathing well? Talking loud and clear? I think those machines are making no difference. Maybe you don't even need them any more, don't you think?

The young woman was surprised, paused for a moment, certainly checking her own condition, then said:

"You're right, you're right... I'm fine..."

(As she had disincarnated, she no longer needed oxygen to breathe.)

So, those who are taking care of you know what they're doing. Trust them, you're in good hands...

At that moment, she remarked:

"Someone is coming in. It's the nurse..."

(Actually, it was a spirit rescuer which presented itself wearing a hospital uniform to carry on attending to the young woman, who was calmer now. The connection of the young woman's spirit with the medium had served to make her listen to us and drop that fixed idea she had brought, which had fortunately been achieved.)

Feeling calm and safe, exhausted with the distress she had felt, the young woman then relaxed and said:

"I'm sleepy..."

She was about to enter into restful sleep in a proper environment on the spiritual plane. She was told to sleep quietly because she was protected, but that she should thank God for the help she had received, as we should always thank God, who loves us and provides everything for our good.

She still requested though:

"Please call my mother, tell her that I'm fine and she shouldn't cry any more."

She'll be informed. God bless you!

Her mother would certainly be informed spiritually, even if she was not conscious of that as an incarnate spirit.

For our part, we have no means to fulfill requests like that, nor is it necessary that we do so because the divine providence has established other usual means of communication, even without the help of psychic mediums.

Such communication is passed along the wires of thought, which always unite mutually friendly or akin spirits, whether they be incarnate or disincarnate.

Besides, if a more direct communication is needed or deserved (by the standards of the spiritual realm and not just because we want it), the incarnate, during his or her sleep, may have an out-of-body experience and go visit their loved ones in the hereafter (which enables them to have special, comforting dreams), or conversely the spirits are allowed to visit the incarnate.

13
SUICIDE "FOR LOVE"

When we made the initial greeting, the spirit showed itself annoyed, not wanting to hear anything. We did not yet know what its problem was. When we spoke of divine goodness, it replied:

"His goodness, where? Then why doesn't He let me go back?" And grudgingly confessed:

"Yes, I killed myself, but it was because I wanted her to suffer, to be sorrowful."

And then, frustrated, concluded:

"But she didn't!..."

It would seem that the woman was neither cold nor indifferent; she just did not feel guilty about his action and therefore had faced the fact with equanimity.

His suicide had not been "for love," but rather to avenge his wounded pride, a desire to hurt the woman and constrain her to reciprocate his feelings.

Allow me to make a parenthesis to explain:

Many times the spirit of a suicide, besides facing hard and painful consequences in the hereafter, feels stuck to the decomposing body or suffers harassment from malevolent spirits which laugh at their suffering, further increasing its torment.

In this specific case, however, the spirit's suffering was more due to the impossible longing to return and the frustration of not having achieved its purpose of making the loved one suffer. How long had it been in that state? We do not know.

The differing situations and consequences of a suicide in the hereafter stem from the divine laws which are wise and merciful, and which consider, in each individual case, the motivations, the spirit's degree of knowledge, and the disturbing influences it may have suffered.

Knowing now what the problem of the communicating spirit was, I sought to comfort and guide it somehow. But it kept insisting:

"No, I need to come back and tell her that I love her. Tell God that I need to come back! There must be a way..."

There's no way of you coming back to your body, but there are indeed means of communication between the material and spiritual worlds, provided for by God. Calm down, follow the guidance of those spirit friends which are helping you and a solution will come. Don't be rebellious again, as it can further complicate your situation...

I was still talking when the spirit muttered, moved:

"It's her! She's praying for me! I can hear it... She doesn't hate me, she prays to God for me, she loves me!..."

The spirit friends had established a mental communication between them both, so that he could hear the prayer she was making on his behalf. And the spirit then cleverly deduced:

"That means I can also talk to her! She's going to listen to me..."

Yes, along the wires of thought, through prayer, whenever it's appropriate and when you're allowed to. See? All is not lost. You'll be able to recover and resume the good path. Give thanks to God and follow the guidance of those good spirit friends.

"Yes, yes... I'm going with them..."

And there went the spirit, comforted and invigorated by the charitable action of the good spirits which, here and in the hereafter, rescue the afflicted and the suffering, in the name of the love of God and as Jesus taught us.

14
IT WAS NOT HEAVEN...

Reacting to the brotherly initial greeting made by the dialoguer, the communicating spirit asserted:

"I'm fine. What a wonderful garden!"

And went on to describe a place full of flowers of various species, leafy trees, singing birds... In short, a beautiful place of great calm and tranquility. Then the spirit concluded:

"I need nothing. I'm at peace and very happy. Try finding other people to talk to, maybe they need it more than I do. I feel in heaven, because the thing I love most is nature. This is exactly how I hope to feel when I die."

Such vision was not real. It was just a mental projection, a fixed idea cultivated by that woman's spirit. We realized it when suddenly she exclaimed:

"What's this? Everything is fading away! My paradise!"

And, in a panic, she said:

"What's happened? Are you demons and have destroyed my heaven? What will become of my life now?"

No, we aren't demons, we're your brothers and sisters in Christ. You were living in a fictitious, imaginary state, created by your mind. It would have been harmful for you to remain like that indefinitely. For that reason, Jesus' messengers have interfered with your mental projection.

"It was so beautiful! I was so happy..."

But it wasn't real, sister. You need to wake up from that illusion. You think that life in the spiritual world is one of idle repose? Jesus said, "*My Father is still working, so I am working, too.*"

"So I'll have to work? I thought I was going to rest..."

God makes nothing idle. He didn't create us to do nothing, just to live a contemplative life. He wants us to be active and useful, don't you think?

"Yes, might be... But in what can we, devoid of a body, still work?"

Every useful occupation is work. The afterlife is the continuity of experiences of progress and achievements as here on Earth, only on a plane different from the material one. There, spirits are engaged in various activities: They study, work, help the needy and bond together, and also prepare themselves for future reincarnations.

Then the dialoguer, calmly and deliberately providing details that were within the reach of the spirit's understanding, suggested:

Please look around. Can you see anything now?

"Yes, I can see it now. It's so busy! There's a lot of people..."

And there are spirits helping, aren't there?

"Many! See how they work to attend to everybody..."

It was them who brought you here and will guide you to a place there on the spiritual plane, also beautiful and pleasant but real, where you'll be able to learn how to serve, as is God's will. Do you want it?

"I certainly do. I've already lost a lot of time dreaming. May God forgive me! I didn't mean it..."

It was only because you didn't know, wasn't it? But now you know.

"Yes, I know... I'm going with this companion who's calling me. He says he's going to help me."

May God go with you!

"Thank you!"

15

HE KILLED TO FEED HIS FAMILY

In deep despair, he said:

"Where's the justice? I'm not a bad man nor a villain. Sure, I killed, but I needed to feed my family. Then I was arrested and convicted. Thirty years was my sentence. And after all, I was murdered in prison. So where's the justice?"

Calm down, remember God...

"I don't believe in God, He abandoned me! And now he punishes me? Why?"

God is wisdom and justice, He does not punish us, but He reeducates us, making us face the consequences of our actions...

"But why? Because I killed? I was forced to do it by extreme necessity, because I was poor and miserable! And what guilt do my innocent wife and children have to go through all this?"

Wasn't there any other way left for you to earn a living? Many people also face poverty, but they don't kill anybody. We must learn to live without harming anyone, mainly respecting the right of others to life, the most precious gift that God has given us.

"Are you all trying to judge me and convict me again? I've already been convicted on Earth. Why doesn't this happen to people with money? Is this hell, here?"

Nobody is here to judge nor to condemn. We're here to help you. God wants us to help one another.

"So help me soon. How will you help me?"

By showing you new possibilities and a new way..

"But I'm already dead. It's all over!"

No, it's not over. Life goes on and you'll be able to repair your situation. Through ignorance, we create difficult situations for ourselves. That's what happened to you. And the consequences should teach us whether we acted well or not. If we act badly, we'll need to fix things...

"Fix things... I wish I could, but how?"

See, you're free now. So what do you intend to do? We understand that you need to start acting better in order to achieve happier results in your life which never ends.

"Tell me what I can do."

Talk to the spirit messengers which brought you here. They'll guide you.

"What about my family?"

Your family members are also receiving divine help, just like you. They'll be fine. God doesn't abandon any of his children.

Still suffering, but now calmer and hopeful, he followed on with the kind spirit rescuers.

16
A PROVEN IDENTITY

When it comes to communicating with spirits, one of the most desired goals seems to be the proof of identity, because it confirms the existence and immortality of the spirit in the preservation of their individuality.

In our Spiritist Center, there occurs sometimes spontaneous communications in which the spirits, whether they be known to us or not, provide sufficient proof of identity. Such communications can be touching or of great interest. However, they are not usual.

Sometimes, a few spirits seem to want to identify themselves, send a message to family members, but fail to correctly pass us the data for the required proof.

We had been aware of that fact and could not explain the reason for it, yet we deduced that it must have been happening due to some higher ruling for our mediumistic work, so as to prevent us from acting as personal messengers when spirits address their own families, in which case proof of identity would become indispensable.

We understood that, should our Spiritist Center start receiving that type of communication, an extensive line of people interested in getting messages from their deceased family members would then form at our doors, thus hindering or even preventing our daily activities of doctrinal studies and spiritual assistance, provided through interviews, lectures, passes and mediumistic meetings, in which so many people and spirits are assisted.

I personally had a corroboration of what we thought in a communication given by a deceased relative of mine, which I will now narrate. If such communication referred to members of another family, we would then need authorization to disclose its content.

ৡ❀ৎ

She communicated through a medium, complaining that her children had abandoned her. She said she was not angry, but felt deeply hurt because she did not expect that from them.

Another dialoguer was attending to her, but when I came closer attracted by the subject, she called me by my name.

Do you know me? I asked.

"How don't I?"

In a disciplined way, I kept attending to her in a brotherly manner, not letting myself be carried away by curiosity, and managed to somewhat comfort her. Incidentally, it could be noticed that she was already under the protection of spirit friends.

At the end of the meeting, I asked the medium if he had been able to perceive something about that communicating spirit. He described her as a lady, not fat but with plump arms, wearing a flower print dress.

And the name, I asked, could you pick up her name? He had picked it up and told it to me. I thought: Yes, I had had a relative by that name and fitting that appearance. Yet, abandoned by her children? That was not to my knowledge.

At home, I asked my mother who confirmed that fact, but added that it had not been exactly an abandonment. That relative had developed multiple sclerosis, could not recognize anyone and was very agitated. Her whole family had to work outside the home. So they sent her to a good clinic, where she was very well treated, but in fact no one visited her. They certainly thought she would not notice it, for being mentally alienated.

However, we now know that the breakdown of her physical condition did not prevent her from knowing, spiritually, that her children were not visiting her, and she took it as abandonment.

This fact serves as a lesson to all of us, in order to be more careful when dealing with people who may seem to be unaware of what is going on around them, but spiritually are aware of what is happening, only not able to express it correctly because their bodies do not allow it.

At the following mediumistic meeting, I was attentive to the communications given through the medium who had channeled my relative. Who knows, maybe she would come again? And she did, presenting herself more composed; and when I greeted her, she said my name again.

So you know me...

"Of course!"

Then please tell me your name.

(It was then that, through the medium, she made a slight pause, tilted her head to my side and whispered:)

"They don't want me to say it. There are many strangers here…"

I realized that for my relative, an uneducated woman, that was the way the spirit friends had found to prevent an unnecessary identification which would call everyone's attention, since the essential – her individuality, the family facts – had already been established.

Also it had been proved that it is through the interference of spirit mentors that, in our Spiritist Center, the communicating spirits do not usually identify themselves.

The main objective of the communications in the services maintained by CEAK is not any personal messaging, but rather the reception and assistance to spirits that the On-High sends to us in order to be brotherly assisted.

Daily, they come to our meetings. And they are many! Anonymous and unknown they arrive, and unknown and anonymous they leave; yet now comforted and enlightened, or warned and invited to do good, as our fellow beings in Christ, which they all are.

17

ACTING UNDER THE ORDERS OF OTHERS

"No, I won't go! I won't! I won't! Who do you think you are?!"

Where do they want you to go?

"They want me to stop doing what I was tasked to do. They're claiming that I won't have any advantage, that I'm wasting my time and, no matter what I do, the results will always escape my control. And what have I got to do with it? I don't have to know of any results, I don't want to control anything, I just want to do what I was told to do, that's all! You think you'll go far with these things you do here? They're worthless! You know nothing!"

You say you're fulfilling commitments that you made. But we're all children of God, the Creator, and our greatest commitment is always to God, the Divine Creator. He who created us and sustains us... Who gives us life?

"I have nothing to do with all that."

Of course you have, you're a son of God. You have to think of your Father, your Creator, how don't you? The others are the others, but God is the Creator, the Father, you can't forget Him. Somebody gave you a task... Now, is that task good, does it make any progress for you? If it won't give you peace and prosperity in the future, it won't serve you! How do you accept an assignment like that?

Just because people are offering you some advantage? No, the greatest advantage is that which God gives us. He gives us affective ties, true friends, a family... Because you won't be able to stay forever there, where you are, you'll have reincarnate, won't you? You know that, don't you?

"I don't know if that story you're telling is true. I won't come back, not me, I won't come back, no way!"

But we all have to come back, it's a divine law, you know?

"No way I'll come back! Who do you think you are? You think you can give me orders? You think you..."

We don't want to give you orders. We speak to you as we speak to ourselves. We say: Look, think of God, see God's law, don't do anything that's going to result in problems for yourself... That's the way we speak to ourselves, and that's the way we're speaking to you. Except that you aren't alerted to this. You're away from your loved ones, those who always treated you well, who didn't fail you... If they were here, they'd be counseling you too, don't you think? They'd be sincere, your friends wouldn't deceive you, wouldn't try to exploit what you can do... Think hard! You have to find a worthy and healthy life, a life of progress... And you can, of course you can!

"What will they gain from all this, huh?"

Nothing! It's just that we've learned that we have to love our fellow beings. It's no use doing evil to fellow beings, because it returns to us. It's the law of cause and effect.

"You guys must have done a lot of bad things because you have no idea how many enemies are now wanting to set traps on your way..."

Sometimes it's not that we've done anything wrong. True, way back in the past, none of us was quite perfect, but now we're willing to do good. And when we want to do good, sometimes we hinder the purposes of those wanting to do evil, and they dislike our interference. But we wish well to everyone, we wish no one any harm.

"Then let's end this conversation. I've already understood it."

I really wish you had the opportunity to see someone dear to you again, someone sincere and friendly. We pray to God that this be so and you may finally rest your heart in a friend's heart. May God bless and protect you! And may God get it for you, because deep down you're not evil, you don't want to do bad things. It's just that you haven't seen another way yet. But there's a much better way...

"So tell me. If I jump to your side of the fence, what are you guys going to give me? What will I gain?"

We don't give anything to anyone, not even to ourselves. It's the divine law that gives...

"Then how am I going to 'jump'?..."

If you come to this side, you'll begin to get rid of bad company and find friendly company; you'll learn to make good things which won't cause you problems... You'll grow and progress... After all, you have a right to it. Why would you live forever in such a state as you are? No! You're going to improve! Here on Earth don't we usually say *Get closer to the good and you'll become one of them?*[17] So, you're being invited: Get closer to the good and you'll become one of them...

"Are you going to arrest me?"

No, there's no prison...

"Because here I'm a prisoner, I can't get out..."

Oh, but if you came here, brought by the spirit friends, it's because the opportunity is yours to start a new life. You're not alone, nor abandoned. If you will, there's a new path right there ahead of you. A good environment, new and better things for you to know... You only have to want it!

"Yeah, I know... They tell me so many things I've lost count..."

You can see those spirit friends out there, can't you?

"Yes, I can. It's full of guards holding me back here..."

They aren't just guards, they're friends. They maintain security, of course, otherwise evil people would try to do some harm... But these guards are not here to mistreat others, they're here to defend those who want to do good. You'll have this defense too, if you want it.

"So, you're not going to arrest me..."

No, we're just inviting you...

17 [Trans. note] A Luso-Brazilian saying based on a Latin proverb.

"Then I'm going to check what this is all about... But I'm making no commitment!"

Right, you have free will, you'll always be free. But it will be good if you acknowledge...

"It's your call, if you want me to stay, I'll stay."

We certainly do. Those friends brought you here to help you. It's the divine law, to help one another.

"There's a lot of people here, so much anchorage..."

God bless you! Please stay with these spirit friends which will escort you. Also know, observe and receive all the good things they'll offer you, so that you have a better feeling and feel safe...

"I'm going to check what this is all about."

God bless you! We're very pleased that you've accepted our invitation.

"All right..."

18

SURPRISE IN THE HOSPITAL

The spirit thought it was lying in a hospital bed and that the dialoguer had just entered its room. Then it remarked:

"I think someone has turned off the machine. I can't breathe..."

Are you alone?

"Yes."

Try to keep calm, I'm going to help you right away. Can you ring the bell?

"No, I feel strange, as if I were floating above my body..."

How is that feeling?

"It's good, I no longer miss breathing. I thought that when I died, it would be different though..."

Different, in what way?

"As if I slept here and woke up there, already in the arms of my old wife. I long so much for her..."

When we leave our bodies, we often need to go through a preparation process and only afterwards meet the people we love, if God so allows.

"Why am I stuck to my body and can't go out?"

You want to go out?

"I do, I'm longing so much for my old wife, I don't want to stay here any longer."

Then, let's give it a try. Make an effort to leave now... and walk slowly...

"Good Lord! The doctors have just come rushing in here... One of them is staring very seriously at me and you..."

Maybe he's going to say something, who knows?

"He's telling me it's still not time for me to leave my body, that I should go back right away!"

The psychic medium then regained consciousness with an unpleasant sensation of fright: That communicating spirit was still incarnate!

Recapping this communication, the following is noted:

- The spirit was still incarnate and in a hospital bed;

- He felt somewhat detached from his body, because it was debilitated;

- When he tried to go away, that must have triggered some reactions in his body, alerting the medical personnel who rushed in to assist him in the emergency;

- The doctor that was staring seriously at them was not an incarnate, but rather a spirit which assisted the ill patient and told him to go back to his body.

It was a case of out-of-body experience, where a spirit with its perispirit moves away from the physical body.

While in an out-of-body experience, a spirit may regain its spiritual conditions which the body restricts, and act as a disembodied spirit (disincarnate), going at a distance, appearing to others (visits of the living) and even communicating through a medium.

Those who are unaware of this phenomenon, which Kardec's Codification explains so well,[18] may feel surprised at these communications.

It is because of facts like this that one should refrain from hastily stating to a communicating spirit that it has already died, because it may actually still be incarnate, only in an out-of-body experience, and communicating the same way a disincarnate spirit would.

---

18 Please refer to *The Mediums' Book*, Part 2, Ch. VII, "Bi-corporeity and Transfiguration," 2ⁿᵈ ed., Brasília, DF, Brazil: FEB, 1986.(Trans. note: "bi-corporeity" is synonymous with "bicorporeality.")

19

Everybody wants happiness

Natural and innate to human beings is the yearning for happiness.

God created us for perfection, for the full development of our intellectual and moral potentials and, when we exercise the latter correctly, to produce good in us and around us, resulting in this fullness of well-being which we call happiness.

Although a full and complete happiness cannot yet be achieved at this moment in time in our earthly lives, it is felt in every human being as a true longing. It is because, in spirit, we know that is the destination towards which we are all heading.

Therefore, at some point in a dialogue, the dialoguer may put to the communicating spirit:

What you really want is to be happy.

Responses to this statement will vary greatly: Sometimes an adverse reaction, sometimes despondency or interest, but always allowing the dialoguer new ways to continue the conversation.

Let us look into some possible reactions by rebellious, obsessing or vengeful spirits:

"I'm already happy! Very happy, doing what I want!"

And it may even try to laugh or guffaw to prove it.

Then we can say peacefully:

No, you're not happy, yet...

"Right, I'm not... Only because I haven't got what I want yet. But when I get it, I'll feel very happy..."

That's where you're wrong. That's where you can't really be happy because what you're planning to do is not good. So, if you succeeded, it would only complicate your situation, you'd be caught in the middle of the disastrous effects that you caused... So we pray to God that you won't succeed, brother, because we don't want you to be unhappy.

"You're fooling me, trying to dissuade me from my purpose. Why wouldn't I be happy? I'll have achieved what I so much desire..."

You won't be happy, because to us, spiritual beings, happiness can only come from being in accordance with the laws of God, from doing the best that our evolutionary state allows us. Until we act like that, we won't get the desired effects of peace, of enthusiasm for life, of hope, of affective satisfaction...

(Sometimes we suggest that the communicating spirit note the serene and brotherly countenance of the spirit friends, and then we make the following remark.)

So much serenity despite being so busy. Don't they seem lively and full of enthusiasm? They're already on the good path to happiness, don't you think? We can also take the same path they've found and have been treading...

(Although the decision to accept or not accept our suggestion belongs to the spirit, we will have thus offered it a new vision of happiness and how to pursue it.)

Let us look into another case, this time involving a disheartened, suffering spirit. To our assertion its answer may perhaps be, between sighs:

"If only! But happiness doesn't exist in this world!"

In this world there isn't really a complete and constant happiness, because the Earth is a planet where the inhabitants are either atoning for their past mistakes, or undergoing trials in order to learn something or test their ability in the fulfillment divine laws.

"It's like I say. Who am I? I'll never be happy."

Oh, yes, you will. We're all destined to happiness, all of us! Even those who have committed many errors. And you haven't committed that many. God has created us to progress, to grow "from the inside," to perfect ourselves intellectually and morally. By evolving, we come to understand life better, we start doing what is good and avoiding what is evil...

"Is it that easy?"

It's not easy because it will require constant effort and determination. But it will be worthwhile!

(Again, in this case, we may suggest that the spirit note the spirit friends, all serene and happy despite being there in the effort of serving the needy ones, and then say the following.)

They've already found out how to be happy, and now serve as a model and stimulus to us, because if they've achieved it, then surely we'll also be able to achieve it.

"Well, I don't know... Only if someone helps me, but no one has ever helped me..."

(At this point, we may assure such spirit of the help from the spirit friends, or invite it to pray with us, asking for divine protection.)

In both cases above, we will find that, in response to the communicating spirit's pleading disposition, a spirit rescuer will make itself visible to it, offering it a friendly hand, and the former will be guided to go on with its life.

20
My name is "grudge"!

"Let dormant hates intensify, wounded hearts bleed, the unwary and the unprepared take offence, discord be sown; and let the makers and wagers of wars, of moral wars, stand up in order to hear our voice. May the armies of war fight with weapons of broken, cheated, abused, and lacerated hearts! May the armies of the excluded, the erased, the banned, and the souls cursed by the world, rise up and rediscover this hypocrisy dressed up as peace and beauty! Let they wage war against these souls, all dead for what they call the truth and alive for the evil they have hidden in their souls! Hypocrites! Where is the truth that they say shines in noble souls? I only see lies, corruption, cowardice! Let the armies rise up and our voice be heard. We shall crawl like snakes! We shall sting like scorpions! We shall envenom them with the most powerful poisons, so that, like hemlock, it will slowly paralyze them; the poison that discourages them and paralyzes their activity for the good, the poison that will cause them to become bothered by others and walk away with a heart full of grudge. It is like hemlock which paralyzes from bottom to top until it reaches the heart."

Sorry to interrupt you...

He retorted with irony: "Making me stop my oh so beautiful speech!..."

Oh, but please allow me. It's making me think so much! I'm here recalling Jesus...

"What nonsense!"

I quoted: *Come to me, all you who labor and are heavily burdened, and I will give you rest...*

(He guffawed ironically.)

...Take my yoke upon you, and learn from me, for I am gentle and lowly in heart...

"Never!" he said, guffawing again.

...and you will find rest for your souls. For my yoke is easy, and my burden is light. This is the true path, dear brother, even though we feel hurt and wounded. There's no other way out, other than embarking in the field of love. Because only love can solve these problems.

"This is childish!"

No, it's not, it's the truth. We're everlasting, immortal spirits, aren't we? So how long are we going to stay in conflict when we can improve this situation?

"And where can I improve?" he asked, guffawing.

I ask you to please see; see...

"All is lost and wasted!" he said, interrupting me.

No, it isn't...

"Eyes to see!" he retorted, guffawing

There's much evil, mostly there's much ignorance. More ignorance than anything else.

"The Spiritist Movement thrown in disarray..."

Oh, but it's not...

"It's like the Crusades being restored..."

But Spiritists are doing so much good, despite their mistakes. Many people are being fed, many people are being dressed, many people are being comforted, despite all. Even when someone works seemingly for pride...

"That's exactly what I was going to say. Many sporting a coat of arms they don't possess..."

True, but so what? Whoever receives...

"Is that the truth? Is that the truth?"

Whoever receives the mercy don't take that into account, for they need that mercy. If the motivation of one or the other isn't the most altruistic, even so the mercy of God, the bread donated, will shelter. For God makes good out of evil, doesn't he?

"I was well warned that you're a dangerous woman."

No, not dangerous, just true and sincere.

(The spirit laughed chokingly.)

What danger lies in us finding a good path?

"It's an illusion!"

If it were an illusion it wouldn't be working for us.

"And it works?"

Of course! Certainly!

"Where?" he laughed.

Oh, what do you want, that I stay living here on Earth as if it were a ride? A perennial joy? Or rather you want me as a person like you and all the others, getting back to their feet and developing themselves. So there you have it. We're in transit, we can't possibly want a better world right away. We don't even deserve it, we haven't earned it yet...

"That was not the construction that you were supposed to put forward..."

But that's the truth. Our preferences don't apply. It's the divine law, the universal order. We're children of God the Creator, but the one who created the universe and us was Him. All power is His! And thank God it's a loving power, isn't it?

"So slow, so very slow..."

Never mind. He's slow because we linger, we're headstrong. But if we creatures become more active in doing good... So many, so many are already way ahead!

"So many! Then why not we too?"

Come on! The divine law has no privileges, it's open to us as well. This great invitation...

"It doesn't matter! I'm not interested!" he replied, interrupting me.

But it does and you are too, because you won't find your peace, your fulfillment, in this way. I understand, ah, I think I understand that you have taken this way because of the sorrows, the disappointments and the mistakes that we all undergo along the way. It's quite understandable, but it's not desirable, it's not for the best. All those who learned how to overcome their grudges have progressed...

"Don't ask me that! Not in a million lives! That I'm not capable of..."

Not yet!

"...enduring and overcoming."

Not yet! But we shall be capable...

"I'm grudge personified. Pleased to meet you, my name is 'grudge'!"

Yes, one day, one day you'll overcome... I'm sure of that, as I'm sure for myself, despite my disillusions and my problems... Who doesn't have them, right? But the path is there, the course to follow is there.

"And how do these spirits do it, in the event – in the event, I say," highlighted the communicating spirit, "that some day I might think of, or imagine of, overcoming my grudge. How did they do it, so they may serve as a stimulus to me?"

Exactly!

"How did they do it?"

That's what we have to learn with them.

"Then, come on! How did they do it?

You may observe it. I think you'll have the right, you'll be allowed to approach them and observe how.

"I want to hear it from you."

From me?!

"How did they do it?"

I had to learn it... I think we're guided by our realization, understanding and intelligence. We're intelligent beings who have already tried the other side's way out and saw the complications it brings. And now we see these other friends who have found peace, serenity, joy, motivation and hope... And we want to learn from them. They say the way is that which Jesus taught. He is the way, the truth, and the life...

"Jesus is not a benchmark. I can't model myself on someone who by himself never knew what a grudge was, otherwise he couldn't have been Jesus."

Once Jesus said, *Faithless and perverse generation! How long will I be with you? How long will I bear with you?*

"This is just a whining lament..."

How dare you say Jesus didn't feel...

"That's whining, not grudge. Grudge is bitterness, grudge is betrayal, grudge is outrage. If there's a *tamis*,[19] it can't be Jesus."

---

19 Tamis = a sieve, a strainer; a sifter.

Then see how high was his degree of development, at such level no one could really hold any grudges. And that's precisely the way that we want to head for.

"Since he can't serve as a benchmark, tell me about another one."

He can too, because he's undergone all that before. Do you think Jesus got where he is without experiencing all life's struggles?

"Ah, before..."

Yes, through incarnations. Or should we think that Jesus came down from heaven all ready? Of course not! We don't have this vision of Jesus. We admire him...

"How? Then how, please, comer on. How? How to overcome?"

Let's learn from the Master. Because if he made the way and presents himself triumphant, he's the leader. We should follow him.

"I may concede that in Peter's denial he understood, in Judas' betrayal he loved, in the disillusionment with the populace he accepted those uneducated people; but he didn't have a grudge."

And why didn't he have a grudge? Because he understood, because he knew that those people, despite what they did, were ignorant. *Father, forgive them, for they don't know what they are doing.*

Those people had Jesus, who could help them, guide them, and even so they sacrificed him. Their very hope of improvement, and they were sacrificing him! Ignorance, utter ignorance. Hence the compassion of Jesus. He wouldn't have a grudge against someone who's still a spiritual infant.

"Right, I know many things..."

All those people who have hurt us...

"...but bearing a grudge for having been hurt is not rational, it's emotional."

Yes, but if we begin to use reason... For example, for now the hurt is very hard, very difficult. We then put it aside, block it psychologically, and engage in the best things we can. Why?! Why cultivate a grudging hurt and let it take hold of our life?

"I've lost my personality. Don't know when, only why. But it took such proportions that I've become bitter, and that makes me cruel..."

But all that can be mended... We, the human species, and not only the human race, but all God's creation, have a remarkable potential for recovery. It's what's popularly called "staying power," that's what we, spiritual beings, children of God, have. We renew ourselves. The most beautiful thing I've ever understood is that, should we one day in the future meet two luminous souls – one which followed a straighter path, the other not so – we won't be able to tell any difference between them, because no blemish nor scar will remain. No, there will be no scar left in our soul, in our perispirit, when we recover the way and act with our divine potential. You're going to make it, of course you will! You even have some help. Because sometimes, alone, we surely can't. But with some support... For this reason God has left us the law of brotherly love. We're allowed to help, to share spiritual fluids, mind waves, relief... There's a new world waiting for us.

"But everything is still very complex, as with class struggles, an economy which is not solved yet, corrupt politics everywhere..."

All the same, at this very moment, there's a little mother caressing and smiling at her child, despite all the struggles, so that her child isn't saddened. Love is present. And not just the incarnate's love, but also the love from all those heavenly sets bringing rescue everywhere. It is possible!

"This is ideal, no real."

It's real. The two worlds interpenetrate. Both on Earth as on the spiritual plane, there are those who work for good and those who are still employed in evil.

"I'll stick with the modern thinkers who said that God is a deceptive God..."

That isn't true...

"He must be playing games..."

That isn't true...

"Why good and evil forever fighting each other?!"

That is no so...

"Light and shadow?"

We're spirits created simple and ignorant and now moving towards the light, discovering and developing ourselves... The seed doesn't have any complaints about its Creator, it has potential, and the development work for producing what's scheduled for it is up to the seed: To turn into a large tree bearing fruits and flowers!

"With all due respect, that's philosophy, and one with a medieval slant for that matter. What will we find happiness in, after death?"

We know of the struggles. We know that life, here on this side or there where you are, follows the same laws and, if it's not good here, it won't be good on the other side either. We have to make life good, here or wherever else. Then, yes, it will work. It isn't an illusion.

"You're talking there and isn't even aware that you're talking about what I've always heard: A good life. A good life is that which every human being should pursue, but is nowhere to be found. I used to have a pure soul, I had the desire for good, I relied on human beings and wanted to live the spirituality..."

Ah, you relied on human beings!

"... I didn't find..."

We should rely on God, on the divine law.

"How?!"

Human beings are our fallible brothers and sisters. We must have understanding for them... Prevent them from hurting us, but also us from hurting them.

"*You relied on human beings...*" he repeated thoughtfully.

There's this beautiful image of a dear little mother with a child in her arms, while the child in his ignorance keeps pulling his mother's hair or reaching for her eyes with his little hand... The wise mother restrains the child, while still loving him. We can't be naïve.

"Right, *you relied on human beings...* Yes, that was it! Brilliant! Brilliant..."

But God hasn't failed, the law remains...

"Indeed. *You relied on human beings...*" he repeated thoughtfully. "It's true! It's true..."

Our reliance is on God. Of course the human being is also a divine creation but it isn't developed enough yet...

"You shouldn't have done that."

What?

"Throw open the light so suddenly as you did!"

But you deserve it. You're here because deep down you want the truth.

I'm here because I accepted an invitation. I didn't think it would be as dangerous as they told me. Charming! *I believed in human beings...* That was it... But to change back to believing in God, that's a hard way!

No it's not, for this God that humans invented doesn't satisfy me either. I'm beginning to discover the real God, the thinking which sustains the Universe. And these kind, higher order spirits, they showed me some things that have made me think. So, it's been possible to believe in God, rely on God, despite the struggles and difficulties, and the failures of the environment in which we live. And ours too, because if we were really perfect beings, fully developed, how much wisdom we would have, how much love and capacity for action! Then nothing would be a problem for us.

"Not even the grudge..."

Not even the grudge. Nothing! So are those who are called "angels of the Lord." Though they weren't created perfect, they're at that stage of development now. And that's how I want to be, and I think you too, so as to love without suffering, find happiness in the good you accomplish, in the realization of where it all goes, of what path we are walking on. Even today I was reading that page by Vinicius[20] called "Destiny." He talked about what destiny really is from the Spiritist viewpoint.

"Which is...?"

A destiny of unceasing improvement. And when we develop those qualities, we can enjoy them, creating peace and happiness for ourselves and around us. This is the destiny that God has made for us.

"I've heard so many things in this Spiritist Center, but that one I've never head before."

Sometimes it's not possible to pass all information to the general public. We speak of the Gospel, quote passages, encourage the practice of good, alert to certain

---

20 Pseudonym of Brazilian Spiritist writer Pedro de Camargo.

behaviors... But you have intelligence and that very desire to understand...

"Can you imagine what it must feel to be close to my presence? Terrible! Because if someone feels what I am... It's so curious because it's like this: I watch people and the struggles in their relationships. When there's a small annoyance, nothing important, nothing!... When a small setback occurs, I just choose which side to stand by. The mere fact that I stand by the upset party – who wasn't even thinking about it any more – causes that annoyance to gain such a force, through what emanates from me, that the unfortunate person can't even figure why he or she's being tormented that way. Can you imagine what I am, the damage?..."

Yes, but I imagine...

"And you fling the sun of truth wide open now?"

But I imagine you stay suffering as well. Because while you do that, live like that, you can't find peace, hope, a good disposition. And you need it. The moment you find this path, your presence will be good for others.

The spiritual resilience of human beings is amazing! God has always given a safety margin. We can do wrong only up to a point, from there it's the restart, the way out, the climbing out of the bottom of the pit.

"Right..."

Those spirit friends which brought you here, they have much more to tell you and to show you.

"If you knew... If you knew how it was for me to come over here... Right... Right... That's right. Grudge... Rely on God, not on human beings. Understand everyone, overcome yourself each day. It's a fine recipe. I's a fine understanding."

That the divine law reciprocates each of your right deeds, each of your right efforts...

"And if your conversation has no effect on me... How will you feel?"

It's free will. I must recognize that people have their free will and that the fruit won't fall from a tree until it's ripe. If not today, it will be some other day. Now, in your own interest, it would be better if it were today, wouldn't it? That's what I tell myself.

"Right, it would be better if it were today. But it won't be."

You have every right. *Where the Spirit of the Lord is, there is liberty.*

"Right, it's something deep, that we have a grudge for feeling a grudge... Do you understand?"

Yes...

"It's so... perverse! Rely on human beings, not on God. Rely on God. All right. See you another time."

See you! We'll be here, ready to welcome you. We'll be happy the day you start developing yourself in everything good that you possess.

21

Hatred binds as much as love

He had been murdered, and so had his family. Now his malefic persecuting actions had turned the erstwhile perpetrator into his victim of today. It was necessary to help them both by releasing them from that malefic bond. On another occasion, we would talk to the incarnate victim, who should also renew himself in good deeds. At the time, it was with the persecuting spirit that we could talk:

Yes, I know how much harm he'd caused you and your family and I don't blame you for feeling that way. However, what good is there in insisting on this vengeful attitude? For now, he's also a victim, but soon will it be his turn to attack you? Until when will you both be in this inglorious battle? Don't forget that we're immortal. To remain stuck like that is to perpetuate suffering for ourselves. Better to break free, to take a new and better direction, brother! Please accept help from these spirit friends!

"No, no and no! I'll never forgive him! He has to pay for it. I've been 'working' on him for a long time, the time for my vengeance is nigh!"

(We had already attended to him in several meetings, and he always kept adamant like that. Then it occurred to me, probably under the inspiration of spirit friends, to start a new line of conversation. I began by asking him as follows.)

For a long time?

"For a long, long time! Only recently I found him disguised in his new body, and I didn't let go ever since."

To me, it seems like you got stuck in him...

"No way! It's him who's got stuck in my claws!"

Hatred binds as much as love, did you know that? And you've been hating him for so long... Maybe you've been magnetized to him and can no longer get away from him...

"Fat chance! I get away when I want. I only don't because I'm watching him and making him suffer."

Well, at least you might try to see if you can really get away at will or if, without realizing it, you're getting stuck to him due to your insistence on harming him. Want to give it a try? Please try to get away, try it now!

(Wanting to prove that it was free, that spirit obsessor attempted to pull away from its victim, but failed and then grew alarmed.)

"What's this?! What's going on?!"

(To this day I still do not know whether the spirit friends took action to make him feel stuck to his victim, or whether he had really got stuck in the bonds of so much and so persevering a hatred.)

Now, more than ever, the spiritual help would be for both the aggressor and the victim so that, in forgiving each other, they would be freed towards further evolution, thus resuming their march of peace and progress.

What a warning to all of us, in communications such as that one! And we remember Jesus:

> Agree with your adversary quickly, while you are with him in the way; lest perhaps the prosecutor deliver you to the judge, and the judge deliver you to the officer, and you be cast into prison. *Most certainly I tell you, you shall by no means get out of there, until you have paid the last penny.* (Mt 5:25-26)

Let us comply with the Divine Master, and be united by the bonds of love, never of hatred!

22

MAKING DIALOGUE WITH HOSTILE SPIRITS

Once, we were praying on behalf of someone, so that hostile spirits would stop harassing him, when a spirit interrupted us:

"Hostile spirits, that's what we are, right?"

For the time being. One day we'll be all companions in life. But we're ready to hear you out.

(This way, without completely thwarting him, we evaded an unproductive debate, because he was "up in arms," while inviting him to a brotherly dialogue.)

From another spirit, hostile to someone for whom we were praying, we heard the following complaint:

"You pray only for him and not for us."

And as he wanted to call him brother, he protested:

"You're not my brothers and sisters, you're only his!"

Then we explained to him:

Yes, we pray for him because we were asked to. I don't even know him personally, you know. Yet, right now, you're the one who's our nearer neighbor, and we have all interest in helping you. What's amiss with you?

(We were thus able to have his attention and make him talk about the reasons he had to harass that person.)

And we learn, in a dialogue such as that one, that we should pray not only for the people who come to seek help in the Spiritist Center, but also for the spirits that may be harassing them, as they are also our fellow beings and require enlightenment and support.

A defying spirit said about a Spiritist person being harassed by it:

"Let's see how it's going to be now. So easy to point the way for others, posing as the savior of humankind. Now I want to see where the faith is, where the Spiritist knowledge..."

I agreed, in principle, so that the spirit felt me to be understanding:

You're right, I think it's been like that for all of us really. For us to truly awaken, it's only when the pain comes, isn't it? For all of us! That brother will certainly need divine protection and seek within himself the best he may have gained.

Then I drew the subject back to the spirit:

Yet so should we, right, dear brother? What have we been doing with our lives?

"Me? Only watching," he replied with irony.

But we can't go through life only watching. Whoever lives, thinks and acts, and therefore sows. And if we sow, we're also subject to the divine law, which pays back to everyone according to their works.

(That way we brought the subject to the spirit and its responsibility before the divine law, and carried on with the dialogue.)

A hostile spirit, trying to evade our purpose to evangelize it, accused its victim:

"She doesn't change, she's still the same bad and cruel person."

Leave her and her faults aside. Think of yourself. We have to love our neighbor as ourselves. Love yourself! What's going to be really good for you before God? And this path, where can it take you? It's not for your good, certainly not, because God *will pay back to everyone according to their works,* and you're acting in a way that will generate something unpleasant. Also we have to live within that which we produce...

"I think God uses me as His avenger," the vengeful spirit argued.

I took this opportunity to clarify:

No, God isn't vengeful! He's love and wisdom, and his divine justice is always beneficial, leading those who erred in their ways to do good in place of the evil they did, thus recomposing everything. He has resources to correct His children, to teach them, so we don't need to become "vigilantes." Nor do we know how to do justice, revenge is what we do, "eye for an eye," we want to repay evil with evil, therefore starting an endless chain of bad things.

A certain spirit had been harassing a medical doctor, accusing him of bad deeds in a previous life when it was harmed by him.

For argumentation, I invited him to think:

Have you ever thought of the people who can receive help through what is useful in his work? Maybe you're causing damage and deprivation to those who could be helped by him as a doctor, despite his flaws. No one has a right to harm them, to deprive them of an opportunity of help and support. It concerns not only you and him. He gave treatments, helped and encouraged many people. We mustn't see only a person's flaws. To be impartial and fair, we must also look at the positive side.

Then I sought to awaken him:

Now you, dear brother, how long have you been accompanying him? Don't think your life has become limited since you decided to accompany him? Your future, your chances of spiritual growth, your achievements towards good... I think there was some limitation, some reduction, some loss for you. And is that worth it, brother, when your friends and the good spirits await you with better proposals of work, progress and brotherly love?

"I won't be converted."

That's not what I mean, I'm inviting you to reflect on your life, your direction. The decision will be yours.

(We cannot, nor should we, force spirits to make a decision, only give them brotherly counseling, help them think towards good, while leaving them their free will before the divine law, which is always just and merciful.)

23
ATTITUDES OF THE "DARKNESS"

Phalanxes of spirits still rebellious against good and devoted to evil, are usually collectively called "darkness." These are spirits at times highly developed intellectually, but not in morals. We need to know how they are and how they act, in order to learn how to treat them in a brotherly way, while keeping the necessary caution in mind, remembering Jesus' warning: *Watch and pray*.

An invitation

It was a representative of one such phalanx that presented itself at a mediumistic meeting in the Spiritist Center, trying to convince a dialoguer:

"Come work on our side, it's much better organized and much more rewarding, there are compensations..."

Then the dialoguer argued cautiously:

I have the right to choose, don't I? I'd rather stay in this Spiritist Center. What about you? Wouldn't you like to learn more about the kinds of work performed here? Maybe you'll get interested...

"I appreciate, but it will also be a pleasure for me to show you all that is performed in the darkness. To hear "things" about us, without knowing them, is not the best way. Come check them with your own eyes and decide later. If you're completely sure of what you want, then there's no reason to refuse my invitation."

(The dialoguer did not seem to know what to say. However, he could have argued that we already know the darkness, because we had once been through it, as we evolved from ignorance, which produces what we call evil, to knowledge, which brings us the light of good. We already know suffering and the futility of wanting to act against divine law; and now, though still beginners, we are aware that only love builds up.)

Seeing the dialoguer's hesitation, the emissary of darkness insisted::

"Tonight, I'll come fetch you to know the darkness. You'll leave there amazed!"

The dialoguer hedged around it:

Only what God thinks is best will happen, brother. Go in peace!

A record in a register

In view of the dialoguer's silence after his initial greeting, the communicating spirit said impatiently:

"Are you going to start talking or not?"

(Maybe the spirit was expecting an attempt at "indoctrination" by the dialoguer who instead replied as follows.)

I'm sorry, I'm here to have a conversation...

"And you stay there staring at me and say nothing?!"

I was waiting for you to speak first.

"What's your function here?"

I work as a dialoguer, at the moment.

"But that's nothing! Is that all you do?"

I know it's not much, but I'm a beginner. Maybe soon I'll be able to do a little more.

"It's pretty bad, you got to improve..."

(Through the medium, the spirit took a stance as if writing down everything the dialoguer was saying, then returned to the charge.)

"Is there anything else that you remember doing or intend to do?"

No, nothing I can remember at the moment...

"All right then."

(At this point, still through the medium, the spirit gestured as if stamping a piece of paper, then said.)

"All done, you've been registered."

Then the medium returned to his normal state, because the communicating spirit had left. What importance would that spirit's quick communication and "weird" conversation have? What had the dialoguer been registered for?

It served to show us that the phalanxes of darkness are always examining the workers of the good, to know how they are, what they do, what failures they may have, so as to try to act on them.

Should the dialoguer be fearful? Should we be afraid of that "register"? Not at all. It is of no particular concern since we know that temptations and evil suggestions are part of our evolutionary struggles, so that we resist them and thereby acquire experience and grow in goodness.

Provided we are watchful and attentive, and always engaged in good deeds, it will not matter if the "darkness" keeps a "register" of us because, on the other hand, our names will also be *written in heaven* (Lk 10:20), as servants of the Lord, under the protection and assistance of good spirits.

24

CONJOINED TWINS IN THE AFTERLIFE

A spirit felt trapped, totally restrained, not able to move freely. But it was not desperate, it seemed resigned to suffering.

Knowing that, in the afterlife, the spirit sometimes keeps the conditioning of states experienced while in the physical body, or due to hypnotic suggestions, I sought to encourage it to break free from the constraint it felt, with the following suggestion:

For sure, you'll be able to move yourself freely. God is our Father who loves us all and doesn't want us to suffer indefinitely, to no avail. This limitation you're experiencing will end. Take heart and be of good cheer...

"I can't, I can't! I've been like this for a long time... joined to him..."

At first, I thought it was some kind of spiritual dependence and tried to hearten the spirit again:

It doesn't matter how long it's been happening, everything has a time to finish, this time has come for you... Do you believe in God?

"Yes, I do... But there's no way to set me free! We were born this way, glued to each other..."

I got surprised by that remark but soon realized what that spirit's condition was: he had been a conjoined twin when incarnated.

And he still felt that way in the afterlife? Why had he not freed himself?

It was because the problem which had joined them, perispirit to perispirit, and had influenced the defective formation of their bodies in their incarnation, making them conjoined twins, had not been resolved yet. For that reason they remained joined through their perispirits.

I kept encouraging the spirit to trust in divine mercy, prayed for it, asking God to release it; and it obtained some freedom of movement, as it was unable to before.

The spirit showed signs of relief and moved his arms and hands through the medium. But it still felt joined to the other spirit and then complained:

"He's enraged and mistreats me..."

I affirmed that the other spirit would also receive divine help, and began to pray for it. Shortly thereafter, the communicating spirit said happily:

"He fell asleep!... He fell asleep..."

This brought it some relief and calm, but worried that our voices would wake up the other spirit as we progressed in conversation, it asked in whispers:

"Stop talking, stop talking! He might wake up..."

Assuring it of continuing divine protection and the rescuing by spirit friends, I got him to trust and await the support which I was referring to. And at last he felt free, separate from the other, and was promptly sent for the necessary hospitalization by spirit rescuers on the fluidic plane, while the medium returned to normal.

Next we thought of the other spirit, which most certainly also needed help, and made a prayer for it, asking our spirit friends to help it to the extent possible.

Although with limited awareness, the latter also connected with the medium. It proved to be aggressive, rebellious, but it was able to receive some help and fluidic restoration through the medium, thus getting some relief for its suffering condition. It was still unable to speak, so it was taken by spirit rescuers to a region which was appropriate to it in the spiritual realm.

Attending to those spirits, we had just observed in practice what Spiritism teaches us:

— In conjoined twins, born with bodies joined externally, or sharing organs, if two are the thinking heads, two are the spirits inhabiting the same physical set.

— Since such spirits are not spiritually alike, each one will show different feelings and behaviors.

— They had undergone coupling for carrying, from a previous life, serious and deep problems in their relationship.

— If they cannot be released, not even by the intervention of science, the purpose of this joining is for them to learn to endure and help each other in mandatory coexistence, so as to eventually achieve their necessary spiritual adjustment, their necessary brotherly reconciliation.

— If medical science can separate them even during their incarnation, it will be because the problem between them is not that deep, or because they have already spiritually improved through the experience they suffered and now can regain normality, and proceed independently.

— If medical science cannot separate them, they should break free from each other only by the end of their suffering reincarnation.

And through this communication we have seen that, even by then, if they have not yet adjusted between themselves, their joining will persist on the other side of life, since the cause for such perispiritual intertwining is not just a physical issue.

However, while one of them remained obdurate, the other seemed to have done its part in the reconciliation, thus deserving assistance for its release and resumption of its independence on the evolutionary path. Also, the most rebellious one has lacked no rescuing relief nor protection of divine mercy, which sees him as a beloved, albeit rebellious son.

25
A GRATEFUL SPIRIT

After our counseling of spirits through dialogue, they continue their evolutionary path in the world beyond and we usually hear no more of them. When they were brought to our midst, we only had fulfilled our duty of attending to them in a brotherly way.

Occasionally, one of them may come back and manifest itself showing improvement and gratefulness for the help it received. We believe that this happens with the permission of the good spirits, so that the communicating spirit exercises an attitude of recognition for benefits received, and also to serve as an encouragement to the meeting's participants, but more especially to the dialoguers, so that they take heart and do not feel discouraged in the brotherly dialogue with spirits – a task which many people do with responsibility and devotion over years, without their names even being known.

So it happened with this spirit which opted to be channeled via psychography, leaving us the following written message:

Today is a very special day in my existence. After so many inner struggles, after so many missteps, I begin to see myself in a different way, I feel more strengthened in my convictions and stronger in my faith.

The joy of the day comes with the permission granted for me to be here in this meeting, and somehow offer you my humble thanks for the shedding of the veil which used to cover my eyes, preventing me to see the divine truths.

It was in a meeting such as this one coming to a close today, that I received support and the necessary fluids for my eyes to be opened and my heart to be transformed, thus seeking to ignite a flame that would put me on the path of light.

Nowadays I know that a spark already shines here and for that reason I have come by permission of selfless companions, to thank you all for keeping this work of redemption and enlightenment.

May you be, as today, seeking light for those who sit in darkness.

An embrace of light to all of you, friends and fellow beings.

BIBLIOGRAPHY

FERREIRA, Umberto. *Esclarecendo os Desencarnados.* FEEGO Ed.

GRISOLIA, Miguel (Org.). Under the entry for "comunicações," in *Índice Geral Remissivo da Revista Espírita.* São Paulo: Edicel, 1985.

KARDEC, Allan. *The Gospel according to Spiritism* (XXI – "False Prophets (8)," items 10 and 11). Trans. D. W. Kimble, I. Reis. Brasília, DF, Brazil: ISC/Edicei, 2008.

_____. *The Mediums' Book* – Part 2 (X – "Nature of Spirit Communications"; XX – "Mental and Moral Influence of the Medium"; XXI – "Influence of Surroundings on Spirit-Manifestations"; XXIV – "Identity of Spirits"; XXV – "Evocations"; XXVI – "Questions That May Be Addressed to Spirits"; XXVII – "Contradictions and Hoaxings"). Trans. A. Blackwell. 2nd ed., Brasília, DF, Brazil: FEB, 1986.

_____. *The Spiritist Review – Journal of Psychological Studies.* Years 1858, 1859, 1860...Trans. J. Korngold. New York: USSC, 2015-2016.

LUIZ, André (spirit), Francisco C. Xavier and Waldo Vieira (mediums). *Disobsession.* Trans. T. Stevanin, J. Korngold and M. Levinson. New York: SAB, 2003.

MIRANDA, Hermínio C. *Diálogo com as Sombras.* Rio de Janeiro: FEB, 1984.

PEREIRA, Vanderley. *Como Doutrinar os Espíritos.* Fortaleza: FEEC, 1997.

PINHEIRO, Luiz Gonzaga. *Diário de um Doutrinador.* Capivari, SP: EME, 1998.

Made in United States
Orlando, FL
16 February 2022